OCT   2014

Art M

The World
Trade Center

Other titles in the *History's Great Structures* series include:

The Eiffel Tower
The Great Wall of China
The Medieval Castle
The Parthenon of Ancient Greece
The Roman Colosseum
Shakespeare's Globe Theater

History's Great STRUCTURES

The World Trade Center

Adam Woog

ReferencePoint Press®

San Diego, CA

© 2014 ReferencePoint Press, Inc.
Printed in the United States

For more information, contact:
ReferencePoint Press, Inc.
PO Box 27779
San Diego, CA 92198
www.ReferencePointPress.com

LIBRARY OF CONGRESS CATALOGING-IN-PUBLICATION DATA

Woog, Adam, 1953-
  The World Trade Center / by Adam Woog.
    pages cm. -- (History's great structures series)
  Includes bibliographical references and index.
  ISBN-13: 978-1-60152-544-4 (hardback)
  ISBN-10: 1-60152-544-3 (hardback)
1. World Trade Center (New York, N.Y.)--Juvenile literature. 2. Skyscrapers--New York (State)--
New York--Juvenile literature. 3. September 11 Terrorist Attacks, 2001--Juvenile literature.
4. New York (N.Y.)--Buildings, structures, etc. I. Title.
  NA6233.N5W679 2013
  725'.2097471--dc23
                                                                    2013011852

CONTENTS

IMPORTANT EVENTS IN THE HISTORY OF THE WORLD TRADE CENTER

1958
Financier David Rockefeller revives plans for an international trade center.

1993
Terrorists explode a huge car bomb in the underground parking garage, killing six people and causing extensive damage.

1963
Activists lose a lawsuit designed to stop construction of the buildings.

1972
The first major tenants move into the still uncompleted towers.

1960　　1970　　1980　　1990

1964
Supporters unveil the final plan for the complex, including twin towers designed by architect Minoru Yamasaki.

1975
The South Tower's observation deck opens.

1973
The World Trade Center formally opens.

1966
Preparation of the site begins.

1969
Construction of the South Tower begins.

1968
Construction of the North Tower begins.

2000
The World Trade Center reaches its highest occupancy rate.

2011
Basic construction of One World Trade Center reaches sixty-fourth floor, and President Barack Obama and others visit site to mark the tenth anniversary of the disaster.

2004
Designs for a memorial site and museum at Ground Zero are announced and cornerstone is laid.

2000 **2004** **2008** **2012**

2003
Designs for a new World Trade Center are announced.

2009
Name of complex's main building is changed from Freedom Tower to One World Trade Center.

2001
Two commercial jets hijacked by Islamist terrorists strike the Twin Towers, causing their collapse and the deaths of nearly three thousand people.

2006
Construction begins on the new One World Trade Center, the centerpiece of the reconstructed World Trade Center.

An American Icon

The Twin Towers of the World Trade Center are famous for two reasons. One is a positive reason: While they stood, they were among the most familiar buildings in the world—icons identified with their home, New York City, nearly as closely as the Statue of Liberty. But the second reason is a heartbreaking one—and it hinges on the fact that references to the Twin Towers must use the past tense. As the world knows, the events of September 11, 2001, were responsible for this indelible fact. The second reason behind their fame, in short, is that they no longer exist.

The Tallest Buildings

Perhaps no city in the world is more closely associated with skyscrapers than New York. The Empire State Building, the Chrysler Building, Rockefeller Center—these and many more embody a metropolis that has always prided itself on being at the forefront of urban life. Kenneth T. Jackson, a distinguished historian and proud New Yorker, comments, "The essence of New York is tall buildings."[1]

And tall is what the Twin Towers were—briefly. In fact, they were the tallest buildings in the world. When they were completed in 1973, their 110 stories made them respectively 1,368 and 1,362 feet (416.9 m and 415.1 m) high. This surpassed the Empire State Building's record of 1,250 feet (381 m). The twin buildings lost their status as the tallest buildings when the 1,451-foot Sears Tower (442 m), also known as the Willis Tower, was completed later in 1973.

An Idea Is Born

The idea of a trade center devoted to international commerce had been around for decades. In 1939, as a world war seemed imminent, such a center was proposed as a way to foster peace—nations would have to cooperate with each other to promote commerce among them.

During the conflict, in which America was involved from 1941 to 1945, the idea languished as attention was focused on what became known as World War II. Interest in world trade revived in the postwar years, but the idea for a trading hub did not significantly move forward until the late 1950s. And the logical location for a world trade center was New York City, specifically Manhattan—the island at the heart of the city.

Manhattan was a prime location in large part because America was riding high. The country had been one of the victors in the war and had, unlike many European countries, avoided the destruction of its manufacturing capabilities. So it was poised to become a commercial powerhouse, and New York City had always been the nucleus of US economic activity.

The renewed drive to build a trade center in the city was spearheaded by two brothers, Nelson Rockefeller and David Rockefeller. Immensely rich and deeply involved in public service, the Rockefellers saw the complex as key to the revival of a particular area: lower Manhattan, a once-vibrant locale that had fallen on hard times because financial institutions were relocating elsewhere. Building a gigantic center for world trade, they reasoned, would make the neighborhood thrive once more. The brothers' motives were not entirely selfless; David Rockefeller had recently built a skyscraper in lower Manhattan for Chase Manhattan Bank, in which the family had a major interest, and he wanted to ensure its success.

A New York icon, the World Trade Center's Twin Towers (pictured before September 2001) once were among the world's most recognizable buildings. They were destroyed when terrorists hijacked two airliners and flew them into the towers.

Making the Plan a Reality

David Rockefeller formed an organization to develop and promote a plan. He wanted to demolish an entire neighborhood and replace it with a complex of seven buildings that had at its center a pair of immensely tall skyscrapers called World Trade Center 1 and 2. (These buildings, the Twin Towers, were and still are often referred to as the World Trade Center, although the term properly refers to the entire grouping of buildings.) A location on the Manhattan waterfront was chosen, while architect Minoru Yamasaki and the engineering firm of Worthington, Skilling, Helle and Jackson were charged with designing the towers' appearance and structural details.

Unveiling this plan was the opening move in a process that took years. The complex was controversial from the start, and permission to build it required seemingly endless rounds of negotiation among political organizations, private businesses, and social activists.

There were many reasons for the controversy. Some government agencies were wary about the high price tag and how that might affect their own budgets. They were also concerned about how the complex might be used to their advantage. Notably, the governor of the state of New Jersey, across the river from Manhattan, was upset that the original site chosen for the center was on the opposite side of Manhattan from Jersey. He knew that the proposed project would be the destination for tens of thousands of commuters as well as a hub for subways and trains. So the governor put pressure on the developers to move the site across town, closer to New Jersey, so that his state could benefit as much as possible from it.

WORDS IN CONTEXT
metropolis
A large, important city.

Furthermore, large New York developers were concerned that property values of their midtown Manhattan buildings would drop as the World Trade Center, in lower Manhattan, attracted new tenants. Small businesses in lower Manhattan objected to the obliteration of their neighborhood for a project that would mostly benefit huge companies. And social activists denounced what they saw as a land grab on the part of corporations, a move that would, among other things, limit public access to the waterfront and endanger the environment. And many people simply thought the towers would be ugly.

The Icon Rises

Despite the years of controversy and wrangling, the project was approved, and the immensely complicated process of building it began. Construction began in 1966, and the Twin Towers officially opened in mid-1973, although the first of their tenants—a number that eventually rose to about fifty thousand individuals representing some five hundred companies—had already moved in.

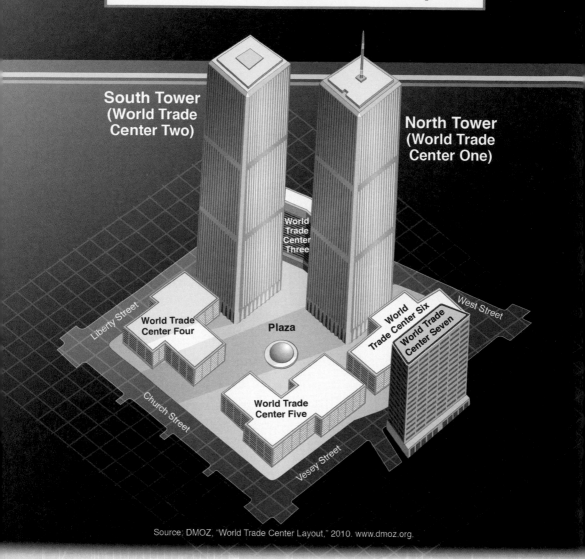

The World Trade Center Complex

**South Tower
(World Trade
Center Two)**

**North Tower
(World Trade
Center One)**

World
Trade
Center
Three

Liberty Street

West Street

**World Trade
Center Four**

Plaza

World
Trade Center Six

World
Trade
Center Seven

Church Street

**World Trade
Center Five**

Vesey Street

Source: DMOZ, "World Trade Center Layout," 2010. www.dmoz.org.

Over the years of occupancy the towers evolved into something more than controversial buildings. Soaring high in the air and re-shaping the skyline of lower Manhattan, the glistening, metallic towers became familiar sights, magnets for tourists, and memorable icons. Writer and photographer Camilo Jose Vergara writes, "They had long since stopped being isolated citadels; they had become a friendly landmark."[2]

The Icon Falls

But then the unimaginable happened. On September 11, 2001—9/11, as it is commonly known—terrorists on a suicide mission hijacked two commercial jets and crashed them into the towers, creating giant fireballs high in the buildings. Less than two hours later the towers collapsed and were gone.

The physical destruction of the towers was shocking enough, but the loss of human life was infinitely worse. The official death toll for the Twin Towers, as of early 2013, stands at 2,753. This figure includes those on the jets; members of New York's fire, police, and emergency departments; and victims who died later from illnesses related to the event. The count remains open because more deaths from illnesses may occur.

The attack on the Twin Towers resulted in the bulk of fatalities on 9/11—but it was not the only terrorist assault that day. Another hijacked jet hit the Pentagon, the headquarters of the US military, resulting in 189 deaths. And 44 more people died when a fourth plane, likely aimed at the US Capitol building, crashed in Pennsylvania as passengers attempted to overtake its hijackers.

From that day on, the Twin Towers became far more than iconic symbols of New York. They—or rather their absence— became emblematic of America's resilience and determination to endure despite its grief.

Plans to rebuild on the site began immediately. And the attacks brought home to Americans a powerful truth: A relatively small but global and determined affiliation of terrorists had declared war on their country.

As a result, the disaster led directly to dramatic changes in how the nation lives today. These changes range from a sweeping restructuring of security and law enforcement agencies to the way increased security measures affect everyday citizens. And the tragedy of 9/11 did not only affect America; the nations of the world have changed as well.

But before the events of 9/11, the World Trade Center had a long and wide-ranging history. Poignantly, this history began because another war loomed.

CHAPTER ONE

Why the World Trade Center Was Built

The origins of the World Trade Center can be traced back to 1939. That year, an enormous exposition, the New York World's Fair, opened in a section of New York City called Flushing Meadows in the borough of Queens. The fair's theme was the world of the future, and one of the exhibits was a pavilion called the World Trade Center, sponsored by a number of organizations including the International Chamber of Commerce.

The pavilion, one of the most prominent features of the fair, had two main purposes. It served as the headquarters for the many trade groups that had built exhibitions for the fair, but it had a broader purpose as well: to promote the creation of an organization dedicated to the idea that world peace could be maintained through trade. International trade, the center's promoters reasoned, would help nations work cooperatively toward a single goal: creating a better society.

The concept of peace through international commerce was especially crucial in 1939 for two reasons. One of these was that nations around the globe were still in the grip of the Great Depression, a deep slump in the economy that had created widespread poverty and misery.

The second issue was war itself. In 1939 years of mounting tension between the Nazi government in Germany and other European nations exploded—and the result was World War II, which eventually spread to nearly every corner of the globe. So the need to establish lasting peace was on the minds of people around the world.

Enter the Rockefellers

During the war years, while global attention was focused on the conflict, the idea of a world trade center languished. But when the war ended in 1945, the concept was revived. In the immediate postwar period, it became clear that global commerce was changing rapidly as international trade rebounded. Karl Koch III, who became instrumental in the construction of the World Trade Center, notes, "Anyone in the business of economics and commerce could see that the war had left the world smaller. . . . The developed world was becoming one huge shipping lane."[3]

America, as a victor in the war, had emerged from the conflict with its manufacturing capabilities virtually unscathed,

while those of many European nations were in tatters. The economic future looked rosy, and New York City was the logical location for a world trade center—specifically, the borough of Manhattan. Home to the New York Stock Exchange and other important financial institutions, Manhattan was already one of the world's great centers for trade and commerce. Urban planner Roger Cohen comments, "Flush with victory, the Americans prepared for a new surge of economic growth. It was evident that the reconstruction of Europe would entail a huge increase in transatlantic trade. To capture these opportunities, the New York Legislature in 1946 created a World Trade Corporation to explore the possibilities for a trade center in Manhattan."[4]

One of the organizers of the trade center pavilion at the 1939 fair, Winthrop Aldrich, was tapped to head this new agency, and an Austrian-born architect, John Eberson, was commissioned to design a complex of twenty-one buildings covering about ten blocks. The idea was dropped, however, when an analysis showed that the center would be too expensive to build and operate. Instead, New York City's available funds for trade were spent on modernizing the city's port facilities.

After that, enthusiasm for the trade center idea flagged for several years, but it never completely died out. It was revived in the late 1950s, primarily by two brothers, David Rockefeller and Nelson Rockefeller. Noting that the centerpiece of the brothers' proposal eventually became the Twin Towers, Cohen writes, "It could be said that if the towers had been given names instead of numbers, Nelson and David would have been just about right."[5]

Revitalizing Lower Manhattan

The brothers were two of the inheritors of the huge fortune amassed by their grandfather, John D. Rockefeller, who had founded Standard Oil. They were also Aldrich's nephews; the older man was married to a Rockefeller. By the time they began promoting the trade center idea, the brothers had become immensely powerful public figures, with extensive track records in finance and politics. They were deeply involved in directing one of the nation's biggest banks, Chase Manhattan. Singly or together, they had also been instrumental in the building of several landmark buildings, including Rockefeller Center and the United Nations headquarters.

Both of these structures were in midtown Manhattan, which, as the name implies, is the middle portion of that long, thin island. Midtown was at the time experiencing a booming economy and an explosion of new real estate development. The Rockefellers, having helped spearhead this boom, now turned their attention to urban renewal efforts to revitalize lower Manhattan, at the south end of the island—a neighborhood of old, mostly dilapidated buildings.

A poster promotes the 1939 New York World's Fair. When the fair opened, one of the exhibits was a pavilion called the World Trade Center. The pavilion promoted the idea that world peace could be maintained through trade.

NEW YORK WORLD'S FAIR
THE WORLD OF TOMORROW 1939

Specifically, the organizers of the World Trade Center project hoped to transform the area around Wall Street which, on the east side of lower Manhattan, had once been the center of the city's financial institutions. These institutions had been increasingly relocating their headquarters to the new, modern, and spacious office buildings of midtown.

As a result, the old financial district was experiencing hard times. The neighborhoods around Wall Street were now mostly home to small businesses and cheap housing that attracted colorful artists' colonies. Many of the older buildings in the area, while full of history and character, had become derelict and even abandoned, and there had been no major construction since the 1920s. Writer Bill Harris notes, "Observers of the real estate market began grimly predicting that lower Manhattan was inexorably on its way to becoming a ghost town."[6]

Reviving the Trade Center

Although the brothers were active in public service, the Rockefellers' interest in revitalizing lower Manhattan was not wholly altruistic. David Rockefeller had recently spent millions of dollars to build a sixty-story headquarters for Chase Manhattan Bank near Wall Street, hoping that it would inspire other large firms to do likewise. Not surprisingly, the financier did not want to see his investment languish in value if lower Manhattan continued to decline.

To this end he created the Downtown–Lower Manhattan Association (DLMA), a coalition of the city's top business and real estate leaders. Notable among its projects was a study focused on reviving the dormant idea of a world trade center. This project would be the first major commercial construction in lower Manhattan since the beginning of the Depression some thirty years earlier. The DLMA saw the undertaking as a joint public-private venture, with the Port Authority of New York (later the Port Authority of New York and

New Jersey) as the center's manager. The Port Authority was, and still is today, responsible for building and maintaining the city's airports, marine ports, and rail transit.

David Rockefeller and his partners made their trade center plan public in 1958. It was a sweeping proposal: a 550-square-block redevelopment program designed to attract financial institutions

⬡ "CRAMPED, DIRTY, CONGESTED, AND A GHOST TOWN AFTER FIVE P.M."

In the 1950s lower Manhattan included a number of run-down neighborhoods and old, sometimes abandoned buildings. Along with hundreds of small businesses and a relatively small number of residents, it was also the home of several large food-related warehouses, including the Washington Wholesale Produce Market and the Fulton Fish Market.

This neglected neighborhood was the area that Nelson Rockefeller, David Rockefeller, and their fellow supporters of urban renewal hoped to revive by building the World Trade Center. David Rockefeller writes in his book *Memoirs*,

> The financial district was cramped, dirty, congested, and a ghost town after five p.m. . . . On the west side, squat, low-rise buildings and warehouses built in the late 19th century were now occupied by hundreds of stores whose dirty windows featured hand-lettered signs for cheap electronic gadgets. The east side was even worse. A defunct elevated railway, slowly rusting away and home to thousands of pigeons, loomed over a neighborhood of abandoned piers and warehouses. Just north, the Fulton Fish Market added a unique redolence [odor] to the area, especially on hot summer days.

David Rockefeller, "To Be a Rockefeller," *Memoirs*. New York: Random House, 2003. Excerpted in *Vanity Fair*, October 2002. www.vanityfair.com.

back to the area around Wall Street. It would contain several buildings, with a single super-skyscraper, seventy to eighty stories high, as the focal point.

To make their ambitious plan a reality, the DLMA held an extensive competition for the contract to design the complex. Two firms won this competition. The primary design team was to be Yamasaki and Associates, headed by Minoru Yamasaki, an architect based in Detroit, Michigan. At the same time, the structural firm of Worthington, Skilling, Helle and Jackson (later Skilling, Helle, Christiansen, Robertson) would take the lead in developing the engineering details.

The Final Design

Yamasaki and his colleagues, working on the details of the design, considered more than a hundred different configurations for the buildings. During the course of extensive discussion and research, the design changed considerably and became increasingly ambitious. The architect and the DLMA finally settled on a complex that included two dramatically tall towers and five shorter skyscrapers.

The primary reason for expanding the project was that the Port Authority wanted a total of about 10 million square feet (92,903 square meters) of office space, far more than had been originally planned. As a result, the single skyscraper became two towers, each with 110 stories. The project's supporters would now be able to boast of World Trade Center One and World Trade Center Two becoming the tallest buildings in the world. Architectural writer Anthony Robins notes, "The idea originated in the public relations department of the Port Authority, on the lines of 'if it's going to be this big, why not make it the biggest?'"[7]

The proposed complex would not only contain office space, it would also include a hotel, an exhibition hall, and an underground mall for restaurants and shops. Furthermore, Yamasaki wanted to surround the buildings with a large open plaza featuring sculptures, a reflecting pool, and places for people to sit.

Brothers Nelson and David Rockefeller, heirs to the Standard Oil fortune, were instrumental in the building of several landmark structures including Rockefeller Center (pictured) in New York. They also played a key role in efforts to revitalize lower Manhattan.

ROCKEFELLER CENTER
NEW YORK
NEW YORK CENTRAL LINES

The final plan was presented to the public at a press conference in January 1962. David Rockefeller called the DLMA's proposal an exercise in "catalytic bigness" and told reporters, "We don't want to compete with existing office space. We want to provide some new use.

A World Trade Center seems logical and it seems logical to have it near the banks that service the bulk of U.S. foreign trade."[8]

Meanwhile, Yamasaki expressed a more idealistic view of the project. He made public his belief that a World Trade Center could be a serious stimulus for international cooperation. He commented, "World trade means world peace and consequently the World Trade Center buildings in New York . . . have a bigger purpose than just to provide room for tenants."[9]

"Just Glass-and-Metal Filing Cabinets"

Some observers had positive reactions to the project. In particular, many people liked its potential to bring prosperity and liveliness to a neglected neighborhood. The plan was seen as an inspiring example of America's overall enthusiasm for urban renewal. Architectural critic Paul Goldberger notes, "It was inconceivable to the Port Authority that there could be anything worth saving in [lower Manhattan's] messy mix of old buildings. Sweeping away the old, and providing a clean slate for the new, was the highest and best calling of city planning, or so the Port Authority seemed to believe."[10] On the other hand, the project had no shortage of critics. This criticism steadily mounted over the next few years as the process of getting legal approval and funding for the project moved slowly forward.

One especially vocal group of critics maintained that the proposed skyscrapers would be so huge that their sheer bulk would overwhelm the neighborhood's existing buildings and destroy New York's beloved skyline. Related to this criticism were objections that the buildings were not designed to fit into the human scale—that is, they would not present a pedestrian-friendly face to the public. And many critics also felt strongly that the buildings themselves were simply ugly and that the towers' boxy design was dull and soulless. Lewis Mumford, a distinguished commentator on urban design, belittled the towers as "just glass-and-metal filing cabinets."[11]

For his part, Yamasaki appeared to be unconcerned with these complaints. When a reporter, perhaps jokingly, asked why the architect had designed two 110-story buildings rather than a single 220-story giant, Yamasaki, also perhaps jokingly, replied, "I didn't want to lose the human scale."[12]

More Objections

A number of government agencies also had serious concerns with the proposed complex of buildings. The project would require the approval of dozens of official agencies and authorities in charge of the city's infrastructure, and each agency had its own reservations. For example, there was the question of who would pay for the work of creating new traffic routes, since the World Trade Center would create a "superblock," and a number of city streets would have to be obliterated. Mayor John Lindsay was a prominent skeptic of the project and threatened to forbid changes in the street layout, although eventually a compromise was reached.

New York's public agencies were not the only groups with reservations about the plan. For one thing, a number of prominent real estate developers were vehemently opposed. These developers had buildings—or plans to erect buildings—in midtown Manhattan. They saw the renewal of lower Manhattan as a threat to their rents and property values.

The owner of the Empire State Building, Lawrence A. Wien, was one of the most vocal of these critics, at least in part because he did not relish the idea of losing the honor of having the world's tallest building. Wien organized a group of developers, the Committee for a Reasonable World Trade Center, to demand that the project be scaled back. Other groups opposed to the project included TV companies. They were concerned that the Twin Towers might interfere with their

⬡ WHY NOT TO BUILD A SUPER-SKYSCRAPER

Deciding to make the World Trade Center the tallest building in the world was a purely symbolic gesture. It had no practical use, and, in an important way, was actually negative. Simply put, in strictly financial terms a taller skyscraper is not a better skyscraper.

In large part this is because the taller a building becomes, the less usable office space is typically available, since increasingly large amounts of space are needed for elevator shafts. Less usable space, in turn, cuts into the building owner's rental profits. Goldberger comments, "It made little sense to build towers much higher than . . . eighty stories. . . . The problem was not engineering—structural engineers could easily produce a skyscraper twice the height of the Empire State Building, or more—but economics. Super-tall buildings are astonishingly expensive [so] somewhere around eighty stories, the economics generally cease to make sense."

Still, ever since the first skyscrapers were built the distinction of having the tallest has been important in terms of prestige and advertising. This was primarily what lay behind the New York City building boom of the 1920s that resulted in such landmark skyscrapers as the Chrysler Building, the Empire State Building, and Rockefeller Center.

Angelo Lomeo, Sonja Bullaty, and Paul Goldberger, *The World Trade Center Remembered*. New York: Abbeville, 2001, p. 17.

broadcasts, which then originated from the top of the Empire State Building. (The broadcast towers used for these were later moved to the World Trade Center.)

Two Governors Face Off

Yet another criticism of the proposed trade center focused on the sheer economics of the project. These critics objected to the city's financial involvement in such a huge undertaking. They argued that the buildings would be so huge that they could never be fully occupied and thus would lose money for the city.

But there was a solution to this problem, and it came from within the Rockefeller family. Writer Eric Darton comments, "Fortunately, David's brother ran an agency that could validate the public purpose of just about anything—even the World Trade Center."[13]

That man was none other than Nelson Rockefeller, and the so-called agency he ran was the State of New York—he was elected as governor in 1959. As such, he squelched the economic objection to the towers by announcing that New York State would lease 2 million square feet (185,806 square meters) of office space, enough to virtually guarantee that the new complex could be viable financially.

Meanwhile, the project was running into stubborn resistance from Robert B. Meyner, the governor of New Jersey. Meyner was furious that the location chosen for the project—on the southeast edge of Manhattan, bordering the East River—had been chosen without consulting him. He could see that the neighborhood around the new buildings would boom financially—but that this would not benefit his state, which was in the opposite direction—across another river, the Hudson, from Manhattan's west side.

Meyner also knew that his state's train system was in serious financial trouble, a situation that could be solved in large part by including in the proposed complex a new transit hub between the states. In part, this was because many commuters from New Jersey, dissatisfied with the dirty and inconvenient mass transit then available, were choosing to drive into the city—a situation that meant little profit for the state. Making the commute by train or subway more attractive to New Jersey residents would result in profits for the state-run transit systems. Another reason to move the site, Meyner argued, was that—unless the venue changed—tens of thousands of commuters from New Jersey who would be working in the new financial district would be seriously inconvenienced. As it was planned, these commuters would arrive on the west side of Manhattan but would have to travel awkwardly across town to reach their workplaces on the east side.

Meyner kept up pressure on Rockefeller and the DLMA, and in time they gave in to his objections. The developers agreed to move the trade center site to Manhattan's southwest edge along the Hudson River and directly across from New Jersey. The new location would now take up a superblock bounded by Liberty, Church, West, and Barclay Streets in a neighborhood that *New York Times* reporter Martin Arnold characterized as "one of the city's oldest and most colorful commercial centers."[14]

Public Criticism

Political and practical objections notwithstanding, perhaps the most prominent obstacle the project faced was public criticism. Some of this criticism was relatively minor. For example, bird-watching groups opposed the project out of concerns that the towers would pose a hazard to migrating birds.

Much stronger opposition came from social activists and people who lived or worked in the area where the towers would be built. For one thing, they pointed out, the public would lose access to the area's waterfront. Furthermore, the project would eradicate a neighborhood that was appreciated by many for its colorful history and beautiful, if neglected, buildings.

And the project would have a significant impact on hundreds of residents, the estimated thirty thousand people who worked in the area, and the owners of more than thirteen hundred small commercial and industrial businesses. These small companies made or sold inexpensive products such as housewares, jewelry, stationery, garden supplies, and secondhand items. Of particular concern to those who cherished the old Manhattan was a section called Radio Row, several blocks containing about four hundred small stores that specialized in cheap surplus electronics products such as spare radio parts.

The Port Authority offered to compensate neighborhood business owners and residents by relocating them and paying them cash. However, the Port Authority offered each business only $3,000 (about $21,000 in 2013 dollars), an insultingly low figure, and the vast majority of the business owners refused.

Business owners protest plans for the World Trade Center project in 1962. They feared the project's effects on small businesses located in the area.

Protests

As time went on, public opponents to the World Trade Center project became increasingly vocal in their opposition, staging numerous rallies and protests. At one such rally activists carried a black-draped coffin with a sign reading "Small Businessman."[15] Oscar Nadel, one of the protest movement's chief organizers, commented, "This project is to benefit banks, insurance companies, brokers, people dealing in international trade. Why should the Port Authority put us out of business for something like that? . . . It will take five years to build it. What do they think will happen to our businesses while they are building?"[16]

Opponents to the project also filed a lawsuit in an attempt to stop what they characterized as a "monstrous land grab."[17] The case reached the US Supreme Court, but the court refused to consider it, and in 1963 the lawsuit was dismissed. This meant that the Downtown–Lower Manhattan Association now had the legal authority to take over the area's buildings through the use of eminent domain.

Making the World Trade Center into a reality had taken decades of proposals and modifications. It was not until 1966 that all of the legal, financial, and public obstacles to the project were finally resolved. When everything fell into place, the construction work—a painstaking, incredibly detailed, and immensely difficult process—could finally begin.

WORDS IN CONTEXT

eminent domain

The policy of allowing governments to seize private property for the public good.

CHAPTER TWO

The World Trade Center Takes Shape

The World Trade Center project had by this point survived years of negotiation and controversy, but the challenges were far from over. Now, the design and construction crews had to finish solving countless difficult and intricately connected technical problems.

Many of these challenges had to do with Minoru Yamasaki's unusual design for supporting the Twin Towers' tremendous weight. Traditional skyscrapers had always used steel columns inside the building to support the weight of the floors above. The outside walls of the building had little to do with bearing the building's weight. This traditional approach is strong, but it has a serious disadvantage. Bulky support columns inside the building take up a significant amount of area that could otherwise be used as office space—and thus cut into leasable office space and profits.

Yamasaki's solution was to get rid of interior supports altogether. Eric Darton comments, "To extract the greatest value from your land, Yamasaki concluded, you must abandon the anachronistic structure of the old skyscraper. Instead, emulate the hollow, fibrous structure of the bamboo stalk. . . . Then you can build prairie upon prairie of columnless stories, as high as you want to go. No limit."[18]

The Tube System

To achieve this, Yamasaki chose a technique that is known as a tube system. Although now it is commonly used in architecture, this system was bold and relatively new at the time. It had been introduced only a few years earlier by a civil engineer and architect, Fazlur Khan, who used it in several buildings, notably an apartment building completed in 1963 and the one-hundred-story John Hancock Center completed in 1969, both in Chicago.

The tube system uses hollow steel columns—typically squared off, not cylindrical—to create the building's vertical walls. These tubes are closely spaced and secured to each other with horizontal beams. The result is an enormous, hollow box that has been likened to a gigantic version of the wire netting often used for litter baskets on public streets.

Yamasaki's design called for walls made of these squared-off steel tubes, each only 14 inches (35.5 cm) on a side. They would be spaced just over 3 feet (1 m) apart—so close together that from the outside the walls would appear to be solid.

One advantage to the tube system was that it was cheaper than conventional designs because it required less structural steel. But it had even more important advantages as well. The outer framework of tubes could bear the weight of the building, making interior walls or columns unnecessary. Interior floors needed to support only the weight of the people, office furniture, and other objects within the building.

This meant that the only interior space that could not be used for offices was a tall, slender "box" at the center of the outer box to house elevators, stairwells, restrooms, and service equipment such as electrical cables. Furthermore, since there would be no interior walls or columns, tenants could use the available space—about three-fourths of an acre on each floor—in any way they wanted, without having to structure their offices around bulky columns.

This was a far cry from earlier skyscrapers, which were much less efficient in terms of usable space. It was estimated that the towers would be 75 percent efficient in the amount of usable space within the total, at a time when 52 percent was considered an outstanding percentage for tall buildings. Karl Koch III remarks, "The earliest skyscrapers were designed with a lot of caution and even more steel. Their structural support, jungles of riveted beams and columns, made

The World Trade Center architect designed the windows of the Twin Towers to be very narrow to give people looking out of them from the upper floors a sense of safety. Despite the width of the windows, the building offered magnificent views of the river and city below.

them extremely strong, if not very conducive to dividing up the appealing spaces. The Empire State Building, for instance, is dense with steel framing, and inside it tends to feel like a catacomb."[19]

The Practical and the Beautiful

Like many architects, Yamasaki was fascinated by the idea of combining the art of design with the science of engineering. So the tube system fit his sensibilities well. It was practical in its strength and efficiency, and he also found it visually pleasing.

In addition to the visual elements of the tube system that he liked, Yamasaki found other ways to balance the practical and the pleasing. For example, the architect hated the idea of having ugly cooling towers on the roofs of his buildings, which was standard practice—even though, in this case, only people in airplanes would see them. Instead, he worked with the engineering team to place the air conditioning systems' mechanical equipment underground.

Another example of combining visually pleasing elements with practicality involved the building's windows. The outlooks over Manhattan and beyond would be spectacular; on the other hand, these views would be limited because Yamasaki wanted windows that were only 22 inches (55.9 cm) wide. Yamasaki personally had a strong fear of heights, and he felt that narrow windows would make people feel safer. He commented, "These relatively narrow windows offer magnificent views of the river and the city, yet they give a sense of security and relieve the feelings of acrophobia [fear of heights] that many people experience in high-rise buildings."[20]

Bracing for Windstorms

Deciding on the tube design and choosing the shape of the windows were only two of the design tasks faced by Yamasaki and his col-

⬡ MINORU YAMASAKI

Minoru Yamasaki, the architect behind the World Trade Center, was born in Seattle, Washington, in 1912 to Japanese immigrants. His father was a maintenance man in a shoe factory, and his mother was a pianist. Yamasaki became interested in designing buildings through an uncle who was an architect. He went on to earn a BA in architecture from the University of Washington, making money for tuition by working summers in a salmon cannery in Alaska.

After earning a master's degree from New York University, Yamasaki joined an architectural firm in Detroit, Michigan. His employment there helped save the young architect from internment in a relocation camp for Japanese Americans during World War II. When he formed his own company, Yamasaki and Associates, he remained in Detroit.

Among the best known of his many buildings around the world are three in his hometown of Seattle: the Pacific Science Center, built for the 1962 World's Fair; the IBM Building, completed in 1963; and the Rainier Bank Tower, completed in 1977. They use some of the same design elements used for the Twin Towers, such as slender vertical supports and narrow windows.

Yamasaki died of cancer in 1986, so he never witnessed the destruction of his masterpiece.

leagues. Even when creating a small structure, architects and engineers face countless challenges, and a project as immense as the Twin Towers clearly posed far more problems than usual. Many of them required new and untried techniques, a great number of which have become commonplace in the years since. Leslie E. Robertson, who was a key figure in the project's lead engineering firm, comments, "A list of the innovations incorporated into the World Trade Center would be very long. . . . Most, if not all, of this technology is now a part of the standard vocabulary of structural engineers."[21]

Significant among these was a way to resist the motion that can be caused by high winds. A skyscraper needs to be immensely strong, but it also has to be able to sway slightly to absorb some of the wind's energy. This was especially true for the Twin Towers, considering that there would be no other buildings close by that would be tall enough to shield them.

To address this, the buildings' architecture/engineering team used scale models in wind tunnels to study the problem. The team determined that the towers needed to be able to sway about three feet in any direction. But this was a relatively large amount of leeway, and the concern was that people inside might be able to feel the building move in a high wind.

To minimize this, Robertson and his colleagues devised a system of thousands of cushioning dampers that would connect the buildings' outer walls to the flooring of each story. In severe wind conditions, these dampers would give a little, absorbing the wind's energy, and then move back into position when the wind died down. The system uses the same principle found in an automobile's shock absorbers. The shocks absorb the movement caused by bumps in the road, providing a smooth ride.

A Vertical Subway System

Another major challenge for Yamasaki involved the construction of the towers' elevators. Very tall skyscrapers, by definition, accommodate more tenants than shorter buildings. But this creates a problem. Putting greater numbers of people inside a building means that extra elevators must be available. And elevator shafts take up a lot of space.

Yamasaki needed to provide enough elevators while sacrificing a minimum of space. So he and his team borrowed another technique introduced by Khan, the architect who had pioneered the exterior tube design. Khan had first used this elevator system in his one-hundred-story John Hancock Center in Chicago.

The key to its success was that it did not require every elevator shaft to go all the way from the bottom to the top. Instead, it used multiple elevators that split trips into two parts.

The idea was inspired by subway and rail systems that use a combination of express and local trains. Typically, a subway rider will board an express that quickly goes nonstop to a certain point; the traveler then gets off and changes to a local that stops at each station. That way, people can travel quickly without having to pause at every stop along the way.

In Yamasaki's plan, only one elevator in each building would go all the way to the top floor. The other ground-floor elevators would be expresses to transfer points (called sky lobbies) on the 44th and 78th floors, where people would switch to locals. For example, someone headed to the 60th floor would take an express to the 44th floor, then change and board a local to the 60th.

The result was that fewer elevator shafts were needed, since expresses and locals could be arranged to share the same shafts. Khan's system proved to be efficient and easy to navigate, and most very tall skyscrapers built in subsequent years have used the same idea.

The Bathtub

On March 25, 1966, with the design and engineering work essentially complete, workers began clearing the site of the future World Trade Center. The first order of business was to tear down the old neighborhood. A total of 164 buildings were demolished, and five streets were permanently closed off.

A formal groundbreaking ceremony for the new project was held in August 1966, and workers began digging an enormous hole for the towers' foundations. This was not simply a matter of digging deep enough to reach solid bedrock. An incredibly complex tangle of underground water mains and electrical and phone wires had to be avoided—a nightmare project for the construction crews. Koch writes, "Leveling the site . . . was a cup of coffee compared with the next stage—digging it up."[22]

The excavation crews faced another unusual challenge on the west side of the site. The project was so close to the Hudson River that the ground was saturated with water just a few feet below street level.

If workers dug there without some kind of reinforcement already in place, the entire site would have flooded.

So engineers first created a temporary barrier called a slurry trench, following a process that had been perfected only a few years earlier for the construction of the subway system in Milan, Italy. Working in small sections at a time, excavation crews dug a long trench, 3 feet (1 m) wide and, depending on the specific area, 55 to 80 feet (16.8 to 24.4 m) deep all the way down to the bedrock. As a section was dug, workers filled the trench temporarily with slurry, a mixture of water and a kind of clay called bentonite. The slurry was not solid, but it was dense enough to keep water out.

A reinforcing steel framework was slid in, supporting both sides of the trench and keeping it from collapsing. Then workers lowered tubes deep inside the slurry-filled trench and pumped in concrete from the bottom up. This displaced the temporary slurry.

The end result was a continuous, waterproof, underground concrete wall, enclosing an area two blocks wide and four blocks long—a box shape that went all the way around the site, not just along the river side. This box was nicknamed "the bathtub"—although in this case it was designed to keep water out, not in.

WORDS IN CONTEXT

slurry

A semisolid mixture of liquid and particles such as cement or clay.

Digging the Foundation

With the bathtub in place, crews could begin on the foundation proper, which went as deep as the bathtub walls: 55 to 80 feet (16.8 to 24.4 m). Some 1.2 million cubic yards (917,000 cubic meters) of soil, rocks, and other material were removed from inside the bathtub and dumped directly into the Hudson River, just off the construction site. This was a bonus for the city: enough waste material to create 28 new acres (11.3 ha) of prime waterfront real estate.

The excavation process also turned out to be a tremendous boon for archaeologists interested in the early history of Manhattan. Dur-

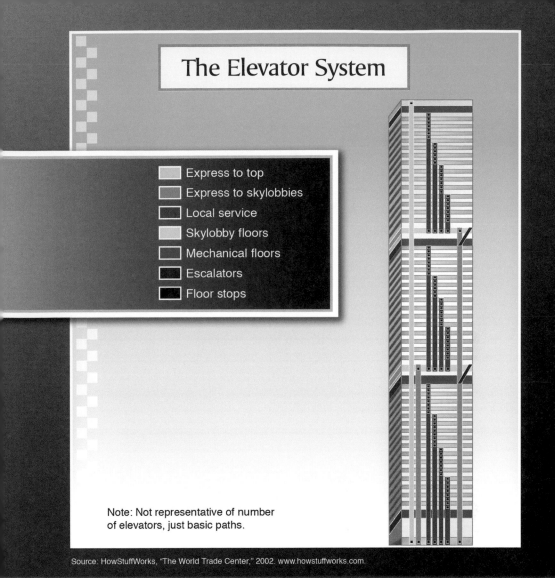

The Elevator System

- Express to top
- Express to skylobbies
- Local service
- Skylobby floors
- Mechanical floors
- Escalators
- Floor stops

Note: Not representative of number of elevators, just basic paths.

Source: HowStuffWorks, "The World Trade Center," 2002. www.howstuffworks.com.

ing the course of digging the foundation, workers uncovered a wide variety of items dating as far back as pre-colonial times. These included pieces of pottery, clay pipes, shoes, cannonballs, and coins.

Once the huge hole in the ground was complete, the next step was to pour the concrete foundation. For this, engineers used a well-tested type of foundation called a spread footing. A spread footing has a much wider "footprint" than the building it supports. The advantage to this design is that it spreads the weight of the building across a wider area and therefore makes it more stable. The principle is essentially the same as that of a snowshoe: The shoe, much wider and longer than the wearer's

"A BEAUTIFUL SOLUTION"

In this passage from his proposal for the World Trade Center design, architect Minoru Yamasaki reflects on his idea for the building:

> For your project, to me, the basic problem beyond the solving of the functional relationships of space is to find a beautiful solution of form and silhouette which fits well in to Lower Manhattan and gives the World Trade Center the symbolic importance which it deserves and must have. . . . It should be unique, have excitement of its own, and yet be respectful to the general area. . . . It should have a sense of dignity and pride, and still stand for the humanity and democratic purposes in which we in the United States believe.

Anthony Robins, *Classics of American Architecture: The World Trade Center.* Englewood, FL: Pineapple Press, 1987, pp. 27–28.

foot, spreads the body's weight out across a larger surface and prevents the wearer from sinking into the snow.

Building the Boxes

With the foundation complete, construction began on the towers themselves, with the two rising more or less simultaneously. A complex set of schedules ensured that each aspect of the project moved forward as efficiently as possible. The many contractors responsible for ironwork, electrical work, window installation, and so on had to work closely together to maintain this schedule. Bill Harris comments, "If one beam or section of conduit [arrived] to the job even an hour late, the whole project may [have been] forced to shut down."[23]

One important aspect of the schedule was that not all of the subcontractors were onsite. Companies all over the nation and in some foreign countries were creating parts of the buildings. Interestingly, several relatively small companies were responsible for forging steel parts for the beams and walls. This was because the two largest steel companies in the world, Bethlehem and U.S. Steel, had revised their price tags significantly up after bidding on the project. Furthermore, executives from both companies had expressed doubt that one company alone could handle such a huge job, and they had suggested that the companies take on one tower apiece.

The World Trade Center's developers were understandably concerned. What could be done if giants like Bethlehem and U.S. Steel could not handle the work alone, especially within budget? Their answer was to leave the two big companies out and instead subcontract with many smaller firms, each responsible for specific aspects of the work. For example, floor panels—each 60 feet (18 m) long and 20 feet (6 m) wide—were fabricated in Missouri and elsewhere, then assembled in New Jersey. This use of multiple subcontractors was more complex logistically, but it was ultimately cheaper.

Another piece of the construction puzzle was to ensure that steel and other bulky components would be delivered to the site at the right time. It was impossible to store everything in the middle of a dense metropolis. Instead, components were kept in a railroad yard across the Hudson River in New Jersey. Much of it was trucked in as needed, with tugboats bringing the largest pieces across the river. Each piece had an identification number indicating where and when it would be used. Likening the process of keeping track of material to a field of battle, the builders called the office that managed this daunting task "the war room."

The Stories Rise

Before anything could be built aboveground, seven stories of underground facilities were built inside the bathtub, atop the foundation. The underground areas included parking garages, room for storage and mechanical apparatus such as air-conditioning and heating equipment, stations for mass transit lines, and space for the largest shopping mall in lower Manhattan. In addition, the underground facilities included ammunition storage for the US Secret Service, which would have a major office in the building; a precinct headquarters for the Port Authority police, and an emergency nerve center for the New York Police Department.

Then the construction moved aboveground, where assembly of the first parts of the building was readily visible to the public. Crowds watched avidly from the street as the outer box took shape. Cranes swung tubular pieces two to three stories high into place, and iron-workers anchored these vertical pieces to each other with horizontal trusses before giving them a "skin" of pre-cut aluminum to create a distinctive silvery look.

The inner box rose slightly ahead of the outer box. When the boxes rose high enough to form a story, that story's flooring was laid. This flooring was made of 4-inch thick (10 cm) lightweight concrete slabs laid atop steel decks and further topped with tile. Then crews completed the floor's interior. Some of this work involved assembling giant prefabricated sections of such features as built-in electrical equipment, power outlets, and heating and air conditioning equip-ment. Other aspects of this phase involved installing smaller features such as windows and carpeting.

One of the biggest challenges during this phase was to find a way to hoist up heavy pieces of steel and other material as new levels were built. The solution was found by the primary steel contractor, the Karl Koch Erecting Company. Koch used specialized equipment, nick-named "kangaroo" cranes because they originated in Australia and because they had unique "jumping" abilities.

Four cranes per tower were assembled on top of the inner core col-umns. Each was capable of lifting 60 tons (54.4 metric tons) at a time to build both the inner and outer boxes. When the job was ready to move to the next floor, the cranes used heavy-duty hydraulics to raise themselves up 36 feet (10.9 m) at a time into open space above the interior box. As one crane did this, another would swing material into place to provide support for the first crane and create the next section of the interior box. In this way, the kangaroos hopscotched their way up toward the sky. When they were no longer needed the cranes were disassembled and brought down in small pieces by elevator.

Finishing the Job

A massive project like the Twin Towers required enormous amounts of human labor. A total of roughly ten thousand construction workers were employed on the towers, with roughly four thousand onsite during peak periods. Koch remarks, "Day by day through 1967 and

The new World Trade Center is shown under construction in 1969. With the foundation complete, all the various elements of tower construction got underway.

into the first half of 1968, the project took on the industrious aspect of an ant farm, many things going on at once as men from assorted companies wearing variously colored hard hats simultaneously went about their respective, seemingly unrelated, tasks."[24]

Perhaps inevitably, such a huge, labor-intensive, and inherently dangerous project was also subject to accidents that slowed the process. Sixty construction workers died as a result of on-the-job injuries. Other serious mishaps could have resulted in fatalities but did not. For example, six workers were injured when a truck hit a ground-level propane tank and caused an explosion.

Another mishap occurred because New York tugboat workers went on strike. With the tugboats idle, the Koch Company needed another way to bring in larger pieces of steel. The firm tried using a helicopter, but on a test run the wind blew the copter's 7-ton load of steel (6.4 metric tons) so hard that it became unstable, and the pilot was forced to drop it in the waters that separate New Jersey from New York City's borough of Staten Island. Fortunately, the only loss was the load of steel, and another way of bringing in the material was found: disassembling the biggest pieces enough to bring them in by truck.

And there were other smaller mishaps, including dozens of inexplicable onsite fires and even a few small explosions. Some observers have speculated that these unexplained events were sabotage by disgruntled subcontractors. Others have wondered if they were the work of activists who continued to oppose the buildings' existence.

"Exuberantly Unstoppable Madmen"

A variety of other obstacles also slowed the process down at times. These ranged from union strikes to winter weather so severe that workers wore two sets of thermal underwear, carried butane hand warmers on the job, and sometimes had to shovel snow off the building's beams before they could start their day. One winter storm was so severe that it knocked down pieces of steel, and the nearby West Side Highway had to be closed.

Nonetheless, the building grew at an astonishing rate: three floors every two weeks. Observing the quickly rising towers, *New York Times* columnist Russell Baker commented that they "seem to go on and on endlessly in the upward dimension, as though being constructed by battalions of exuberantly unstoppable madmen determined to keep building until the architect decides what kind of top he wants."[25]

These "madmen" worked so hard that a topping-out ceremony was held in December 1970 for the North Tower (One World Trade Center), only about four and a half years after the project's ground-breaking. The topping-out ceremony for the South Tower (Two World Trade Center) was held some months later, in July 1971. Those involved in the construction joked that naturally, it was impossible for twins to be born at the same moment—one had to come first.

Construction of the other buildings in the complex had been going on while the towers were being built, and less than two years after the towers were topped off, the entire World Trade Center was officially complete. The complex included the Twin Towers and five smaller buildings. These were designed by architects other than Yamasaki, but they used the same hollow tube design.

The finishing portions of these buildings and other aspects of the complex were completed quickly, and a crowd of four thousand people, primarily Port Authority employees and construction workers, attended a formal dedication and ribbon-cutting ceremony on April 4, 1973. It had taken years of hard work and innovative thinking, but the World Trade Center was officially open for business.

CHAPTER THREE

An Instant Icon

Throughout the construction phase the Twin Towers had changed the famous New York City skyline. The buildings had been provocative from the beginning, evoking an array of emotions ranging from excitement to loathing. Then, as they grew daily, the towers had become even more tangible objects of interest and controversy. Manhattanites could see in front of them what had previously been merely speculation and artist's renderings. *New York Times* reporter Kari Haskell comments, "Even before their official opening in 1973, the World Trade Towers dominated the New York City skyline. They were so big that, seen from afar, the whole of Manhattan seemed to tilt slightly, sliding toward the two silver giants at the bottom of the island."[26]

Watching the Buildings Rise

In any case, love the buildings or hate them, New Yorkers had paid close attention as they rose. The most visible of these observers were the crowds of so-called sidewalk supervisors who gathered at the site every day to watch the progress of the work, fascinated by the scale of the project and marveling at the daredevil construction crews working hundreds of feet in the air. These crowds simply enjoyed watching a mesmerizing show, just as earlier crowds had once watched the Empire State Building as it rose to dizzying heights during its construction in 1930–1931.

Professional architectural writers had also watched the skyline change, and not surprisingly, they had mixed reactions. One who applauded the venture was Ada Louise Huxtable, the architecture critic for the *New York Times*. She states, "From the design aspect this is not only the biggest but the best new building project that New York has seen in a long time. It represents a level of taste and thought that has been distressingly rare in the city's mass of nondescript postwar commercial construction."[27]

Other architecture writers were not as approving. One prominent example was Wolf von Eckhardt, the critic for the *Washington Post*, who initially approved of the design but changed his mind as reality set in and two giant boxes replaced a neighborhood of venerable buildings: "As presently designed, this fearful instrument of urbanicide will not only be the tallest, but unquestionably one of the ugliest buildings in the world."[28] Much of the criticism centered on the old argument that the towers' proportions jarred with the rest of Lower Manhattan. But observers also noted something closer to the ground: The plaza was not user-friendly. Although Yamasaki had hoped the plaza would be an inviting space where people would gather and linger, in reality it was stark and inhospitable. Adding to this uninviting nature was the fact that the wind off the Hudson sometimes whipped through so fiercely that the Port Authority had to install rope railings for pedestrians. As a result of these shortcomings, Anthony Robins notes, "All the life that should have been in the plaza [was] found underground in the concourse."[29]

WORDS IN CONTEXT

urbanicide
Coined word that refers to extravagant public projects forced on citizens.

Filling Up the Offices

New tenants had started moving into the lower floors of the towers in late 1970, well before work on the top floors was complete, so many office workers were already present in the huge new structure by the time of the World Trade Center's formal opening. But the World Trade Center did not fill up with renters as fast as its developers had hoped.

When the facility had been in the planning stages, many skeptics had expressed doubt that it could be fully occupied. For a time after the towers opened for business, it seemed as though these skeptics' predictions might come true. In large part, this was because there was a glut on the New York commercial real estate market when the buildings were completed, so many other options were available to potential tenants.

The planners' original vision had been to lease space to companies and organizations that were directly involved in world trade, but the buildings failed to attract significant numbers of these groups. So the original concept, that the buildings would be a hub for international commerce, never did materialize. Instead, many of the tenants were various government agencies, including the US Customs Service, now the Bureau of Customs and Border Protection; the US Secret Service; and the Port Authority itself.

However, this situation changed in the 1980s when Manhattan office space was again in high demand. As a result, rents skyrocketed in midtown, and large private-sector firms relocated to the Twin Towers. Most of these were financial firms such as banks and brokerage houses, along with other professional firms such as law offices, broadcasting companies, publishers, and airlines. By 1983 the complex's revenues had jumped to $204 million a year.

Contrary to the expectations of those skeptics who had predicted it would not be profitable, by this time the World Trade Center had achieved peak occupancy with all spaces rented out. The Twin Towers housed some fifty thousand people who worked there on a daily basis, representing five hundred companies. The complex was so populous that it had its own zip code. And it had at least one unexpected tenant.

At some point in the 1980s a raccoon took up residence in the ceiling of the underground mall amid a hidden tangle of conduits, wires, and pipes. It apparently survived on food scraps from restaurants in the mall. The animal was often spotted, but maintenance crews were never able to capture it.

The Manhattan skyline at night was once dominated by the Twin Towers. At the time of their construction, some architectural critics applauded the scope and style of the project while others described the towers as giant boxes.

Amenities

In addition to food scraps for the raccoon, there were many amenities—that is, services and features—for the human tenants of the buildings. There were the shops and restaurants in the 427,000-square-foot underground mall (39,670 square meters). Also, the complex boasted nine chapels representing a variety of faiths, as well as exhibition halls, a hotel, and shared conference space.

And the 107th floor of the South Tower was home to an elegant restaurant, Windows on the World. Windows on the World had been initially used as a private club reserved for executives of the building's tenants. But that usage was not profitable, so the restaurant was opened to the public for dinner, although lunchtime was still reserved for executives.

One side benefit—for the city and the public at large—that resulted from the construction of the World Trade Center was Battery Park City. This was the neighborhood built on the 28 acres (11.3 ha) of landfill created when the complex's foundation had been built. Battery Park City has since expanded to encompass 92 acres (37.2 ha) with the addition of landfill brought from elsewhere. It is the largest planned urban development project in America and is complete with such features as high-rise apartment buildings, a high school, a movie theater, and commercial buildings.

"A Colossally Unaligned Tuning Fork"

As New Yorkers had watched the Twin Towers' construction progress and their increasing use as a commercial facility, so did the rest of the world. In part, this was because the towers were, if only briefly, the tallest buildings in the world. But the towers' lasting fame was cemented by the fact that their distinctive shape made them instantly recognizable both to the city's residents and to visitors.

In the eyes of many, being instantly recognizable was not a good thing. The 1973 edition of the *Berlitz Travel Guide* sniffed, "Dominating lower Manhattan (and most of the New York metropolitan area, for that matter) are Minoru Yamasaki's twin towers of the World Trade Center, two 110-story buildings rising like the prongs of a colossally unaligned tuning fork from the depths of Manhattan."[30]

Such negative opinions notwithstanding, the towers were soon a recognizable sight to visitors from other places. In time they became a significant symbol of the city—as instantly identifiable and familiar to the public as such older Manhattan icons as the Empire State Building and the Statue of Liberty.

One way in which the Twin Towers became familiar to the world at large was through prominent appearances in movies during the next decades. Among these films were the 1976 remake of *King Kong*, Woody Allen's *Manhattan* (1979), *Trading Places* (1983), *Home Alone 2* (1992), and the *Superman* movies (1979, 1980, 1983, and 1987).

Good and Bad Points

The sight of the Twin Towers may have been thrilling to visitors, but undoubtedly the single most important reason for the towers' popularity was the view from the observation decks atop the South Tower. This 360-degree vista took in all of New York City's five boroughs: Manhattan, the Bronx, Brooklyn, Queens, and Staten Island, as well as significant portions of the neighboring states of New Jersey and Connecticut.

Enthusiasts noted that on a clear day they could sometimes see as far as Trenton, New Jersey, roughly 80 miles (129 km) to the southwest from the towers. Reflecting New York's traditional rivalry with New Jersey, Manhattanites quickly came up with a response: Yeah, but who would want to see *Trenton*?

Windows on the World (pictured in the 1990s) was an elegant restaurant on the 107th floor of the South Tower. It began as a private club but became more profitable after it was opened to the public.

In some circles the completed World Trade Center was well received. However, many observers hated it. This was nothing new. Long before they were even built, it was clear that—whether loved or despised—the Twin Towers would profoundly affect the city emotionally, financially, architecturally, and politically. Journalist Marc Pitzke writes, "Decades in the planning, often met with hostility, oft abandoned and oft revived, it [had] experienced one of the most turbulent development stories in the history of urban planning. It was an adventurous tug-of-war between political, financial and private interests."

Marc Pitzke, "How New Yorkers Tried to Stop the World Trade Center," *Spiegel* (Germany) *Online International*, September 8, 2011. www.spiegel.de.

And so people lined up in droves to ascend the tower and marvel at the dizzying sights. They had the option of going to one or both observation decks: an enclosed deck on the 107th floor or, weather permitting, an outside, open deck on the roof. On a typical business day, as many as eighty thousand tourists took in the view.

Stunts

In addition to these huge crowds of tourists, the towers' height and fame proved irresistible to a variety of daredevils who captured worldwide attention. Officials of the Port Authority, which maintained the site, had mixed feelings about these adventurers. They worried about liability—but they also loved the stunts because they drew attention to the buildings and helped build their mystique in the public eye.

One such daredevil was Owen J. Quinn, who in 1975 disguised himself as a construction worker, hid his equipment in a duffel bag, and successfully made a low-altitude parachute jump from the top of the South Tower. When Quinn landed, he was arrested for trespassing, reckless endangerment, and disorderly conduct. The parachutist achieved a brief degree of fame—until two others eclipsed him.

One of them was George Willig, a mechanical designer and avid rock climber. In May 1977 Willig—who became known as the Human Fly—scaled the exterior of the South Tower using equipment he had made himself, specifically clamps that fit into tracks used for window washing.

It took Willig only about three and a half hours to reach the top. He later stated that the ascent itself was remarkably easy for two reasons. He had planned the stunt so well, having visited the building several times to secretly measure the window washing tracks. Also, the building was symmetrical. Willig felt that the biggest challenge had been designing the clamps, commenting, "The climb itself was not particularly difficult; rock climbing is a lot more scary because it's so problematical and precarious. I had a solid footing all the way up the building and my route was predetermined, so I had no decisions to make."[31]

"A Personal Challenge Met and Satisfied"

As a huge crowd gathered on the street to watch, two NYPD officers descended from the roof on a window-washing platform in an attempt to get Willig to give up and join them. But the daredevil won the policemen over, convincing them that he knew exactly what he was doing, and for the last part of the climb the three chatted amiably as the officers were brought back up the building's side on their window-washing platform.

Despite his congeniality with the policemen, Willig was arrested when he reached the top floor and clambered through a window. So were two friends on the ground who had helped him plan and execute the stunt. But the mayor of New York City, Abraham Beame, knew that public sympathy was overwhelmingly in favor of the Human Fly, so the daredevil's fine was one dollar and ten cents—one cent for every floor of the tower.

Many people, as might be expected, thought that Willig was not quite sane. But for millions of others his stunt was a brave endeavor that lifted their spirits. Writer Sam Moses comments, "To Willig the climb was a personal challenge met and satisfied, a mountain conquered: no more. But it was more, more than a feat, more than a stunt. It was a triumph of human spirit."[32]

The High-Wire Artist

Willig's achievement drew the world's attention to the Twin Towers, but another stunt created far more publicity and did much more to immortalize the buildings. This feat was performed by French high-wire acrobat Philippe Petit. In August 1974, at the age of twenty-four, Petit walked between the still unfinished towers on a high wire—a distance of about 130 feet (39.6 m), and 1,368 feet (417 m) above the streets of Manhattan.

His accomplishment made Petit an instant folk hero. A Public Broadcasting Station writer states,

> To the delight of the Port Authority, the exploit made front-page news around the world. . . . In the years to come, he would often return to the breathtaking perch where he had captured the attention of the entire world, and, in the space of just 45 minutes, accomplished a seemingly impossible feat: making two of the tallest, largest and most imposing structures in the world seem suddenly endearing and friendly.[33]

Petit's plan began in 1968 when he saw a newspaper article about the towers and immediately fixed on the idea of walking from roof to roof. He spent the next six years planning the escapade, including renting a helicopter to survey the towers from the air and assessing security measures by posing as a journalist and joining workers on the roof.

The night before his feat, Petit and his collaborators snuck up to the 104th floor of the South Tower—the building's highest point at the time. They fired a crossbow with a cable to the other roof. Using this, they passed increasingly heavy cables across the expanse until they could string the 450-pound main steel wire (204 kg) and lock it down.

They spent the night in the tower, and early in the morning Petit stepped out. He spent forty-five minutes in the air, crossing from building to building eight times. During his adventure, he did not just walk—he sat, lay down lengthwise along the wire, bounced playfully up and down, and spoke to a passing bird. He stopped only when it began to rain.

As with earlier daredevils, Petit was arrested—in his case as soon as he stepped back onto the roof of the South Tower. Once again, his punishment was symbolic: He was ordered to perform a free show for children in Central Park. Asked later why he undertook his amazing feat, he told reporters that it was just something he had to do: "When I see three oranges, I juggle; when I see two towers, I walk."[34]

The South Tower's rooftop observation deck (pictured in 1995) offered a 360-degree view of New York City's five boroughs and parts of New Jersey and Connecticut. The observation decks drew many tourists over the years.

The 1993 Bombing

Petit's achievement was a delightful diversion, but offsetting it were several severe mishaps. One occurred in February 1975, when a three-alarm fire broke out on the eleventh floor of the North Tower. Although that floor sustained the worst damage, the fire also damaged the floors above and below. The blaze was put out within a few hours, having caused some injuries but no fatalities.

A much more serious event—one that presaged the disaster that would occur in 2001—took place in 1993. By this time the Twin Towers had become more than mere tourist attractions and symbols. The buildings were now American icons and, by extension, symbols of American culture and beliefs. As such, they were prime targets for terrorist organizations devoted to striking blows against the United States. And so in February 1993 Islamist terrorists detonated a truck bomb filled with more than 1,000 pounds (453.5 kg) of explosives in the buildings' underground garage.

The plan was to destabilize the North Tower and send it crashing into the other building. That did not happen, thanks to the tower's structural integrity. Nonetheless, the underground stories did sustain extensive damage, opening a nearly 100-foot hole (30.5 m) through five of the seven underground levels. Eric Darton comments, "The World Trade Center's vulnerable basement garage became host to a superheated rush of fast-moving air, [burying] its subterranean control systems under thousands of tons of rubble and flooding its ventilation systems and elevator shafts with the toxic vapors of several hundred burning cars."[35]

> **WORDS IN CONTEXT**
> subterranean
> *Below ground level.*

After the Bombing

Six people were killed and more than one thousand were injured, many of them suffering from smoke inhalation. Nearly fifty thousand other workers and visitors were evacuated. Because the electricity was out, most of them had to walk down darkened stairwells with no emergency lighting. Extensive repairs were needed, including rebuilding supporting columns, reinforcing the bathtub, and improving the buildings' fire alarm systems and overall security.

A task force led by the FBI was formed in the immediate wake of the attacks, and within a short time uncovered key evidence about the criminals behind them. The FBI's website states,

> In the rubble investigators uncovered a vehicle identification number on a piece of wreckage that seemed suspiciously obliterated. A search of our crime records returned a match: the number belonged to a rented van reported stolen the day before the attack. An Islamic fundamentalist named Mohammad Salameh had rented the vehicle, we learned, and on March 4, an FBI SWAT team arrested him as he tried in vain to get his $400 deposit back.[36]

Within a year Salameh and most of the others directly responsible for the attack were arrested and convicted in connection with the plot.

However, the plot's mastermind, Ramzi Ahmed Yousef, remained at large for another year.

The 1993 blast presaged the later disaster in ways other than its destructive force. In the aftermath came a widespread show of strength and determination. Only a few offices based in the towers relocated after the bombing. Furthermore, donations of money and supplies poured in, and thousands of people volunteered help and support. Memorials, services, and vigils were held all over the world, and the federal government established a fund to compensate victims' families and severely injured survivors.

It was a scenario that would be repeated, amplified almost beyond belief, eight years later. The Twin Towers had become a significant icon in the years since their beginnings. Now they were about to become an indelible symbol of grief.

CHAPTER FOUR

Death and Destruction

September 11, 2001, began as just another workday in Manhattan. The sky was blue, the sun was shining, and by mid-morning the temperature had reached 68°F (20°C), unusually mild for New York City at that time of year. The official government report about the events of that day later stated, "For those heading to an airport, weather conditions could not have been better for a safe and pleasant journey."[37]

The First Explosion

And then the unthinkable happened. A commercial jet appeared literally out of the blue, flying low over the city. Many people saw it, but the majority probably assumed that it was in distress. As the world now knows, it was not.

At 8:46 a.m. the plane struck the North Tower, ripping a hole from the ninety-fourth to the ninety-eighth floors and creating a giant fireball. The plane's fuel supplies ignited on impact and quickly burned out, but not before igniting virtually everything inside the affected floors, including office equipment, paper, and the building's material itself.

The fire raced to the other side of the building in a matter of seconds—much faster than a typical structural fire. The blaze then quickly spread along the outside of the building and through interior shafts to other floors. And millions of New Yorkers watched in horror as the tower began to burn.

Evacuating the North Tower

Inside the building, the explosion caused terrible panic. No one knew what was happening—but it was clear that it was something terrible and that everyone needed to get out as quickly as possible.

At first the building did not appear to be in danger of collapse, and nearly all of the tens of thousands of people who were below the point of impact had time to evacuate. But as these panicked people rushed to leave, the scene quickly turned chaotic. As thousands, including many with injuries or suffering from smoke inhalation, fled down and out of the building rescuers were desperately trying to get into the building and climb up to where thousands more waited for help.

The chaos was aggravated by conflicting instructions from Port Authority security personnel. Although many people chose to flee on their own, others waited in their offices, assuming that security would soon issue instructions. The security staff, like the vast majority of people observing from the street, believed that the tower was not in immediate danger. Security also feared that overcrowding the stairwells would lead to fatal crushes.

So they told people over the public address system to stay in their offices and await rescue. This decision followed standard guidelines for dealing with such situations, since research on high-rise fires stresses that most of the people inside a building should stay where they are. Specifically, the guidelines followed by the Fire Department of New York read, "Occupants of numerous floors may have self-initiated evacuation, causing almost a mob scene or near panic in stair shafts of [the] building lobby."[38]

The South Tower Is Hit

Meanwhile, in the South Tower, evacuation had begun immediately after the North Tower attack. It appeared at first as if everyone in the

South Tower would be able to escape safely. But at 9:03 a.m., about fifteen minutes after the first plane crashed into the North Tower, another plane appeared out of the sky.

Like the first one it flew in low, suddenly dipped, and struck the South Tower. It tore a gash from the seventy-eighth to the eighty-fourth floors, and like the first plane it set off a fireball and a huge cloud of thick smoke. Since attention on the ground was

Black smoke pours from the burning South Tower on September 11, 2001. After a hijacked airliner ripped a massive hole in the North Tower (right), a second hijacked airliner crashed into the South Tower.

⬡ LEAVING BY WATER

The evacuation of thousands of survivors and witnesses to the disaster was chaotic, but one great help was a flotilla of volunteer boats that spontaneously assembled to take people to safety across the river. The process was spearheaded by the harbor boats of the FDNY and NYPD, joined by privately owned commercial and private vessels. This was a difficult and dangerous undertaking—so much dust was in the air that in many cases boat pilots had to rely on radar for navigation because they could not see.

Estimates of the number of people evacuated by water vary widely, from 300,000 to 1 million. But even the lowest estimate makes this one of the largest maritime evacuations in history. Perhaps only the Dunkirk evacuation of Allied troops in World War II, which involved some 338,000 soldiers, was larger.

by now riveted on the scene, countless terrified witnesses recorded the plane's approach with video and photos. On the many videos posted online, viewers can hear the screams and shocked voices of people watching from the ground. News helicopters also captured the scene, and it was broadcast live around the world.

At first, even after the towers were hit, it appeared as if they might continue to stand. But the fires had caused too much structural damage. Under the intense heat, steel on the stories where the planes hit expanded, twisted, and buckled. These floors weakened so drastically that the building above them collapsed onto the lower part, with each tower experiencing the force of a multiple-story building dropping in on itself floor by floor.

The South Tower, although it was the second one to be hit, was the first to go, collapsing on itself at 9:59 a.m.—just under an hour after it had been struck. It seemed to disappear in a gigantic plume of dust and smoke. It was likely the first to fall because the plane hit it lower down, causing that much more downward pressure from above. The North Tower remained standing longer, but at 10:28 a.m., 102 minutes after it had been struck, it too fell.

The Immediate Aftermath

By this time hundreds of first responders were at the scene of the disaster, many of them having arrived within minutes of the first crash. Among them were members of the Fire Department of New York (FDNY), the New York Police Department (NYPD), and the emergency response teams of many hospitals and local agencies, including New York City's Office of Emergency Management (OEM). Many of these first responders had been off duty but had raced to the site when they saw or were notified of the explosions.

Other disaster relief organizations also moved quickly to the scene. Some were nongovernmental agencies such as the Red Cross. Others were federal government groups, including the Federal Emergency Management Agency (FEMA), the National Guard, the US Army Corps of Engineers, all branches of the military, and the Occupational Safety and Health Administration (OSHA).

The rescuers faced countless immediate and urgent tasks. To coordinate their efforts, a command post was set up nearby as the center for communication among these first responders. However, in the chaos the communication and coordination between agencies was sometimes poor, hampering the efficiency of the rescue operation.

Perhaps the most urgent problem the rescue workers faced was to find injured survivors and get them medical attention. To provide emergency medical help, five triage stations were established around the site, and arrangements were made to get the more seriously injured to area hospitals first.

> **WORDS IN CONTEXT**
> triage
> *The decision-making process for determining the most urgent tasks required, such as medical help.*

Evacuating the Public

In addition to helping survivors from the towers, the responders, particularly the police, also needed to control the crush of panicked people on the streets, nearly all of whom had fled when the buildings collapsed. As word spread, these panicked crowds grew dramatically as millions of people desperately tried to leave Manhattan. The bridges and tunnels leading off the island soon were jammed with cars, so a tactical operation was hastily organized to evacuate citizens.

Although the site was a dangerous pile of smoldering debris, the task of searching for survivors began later in the day. One of the first tasks was to organize bucket brigades. These groups, most of them made up of civilian volunteers, removed debris small enough to pick up and passed the pieces by hand outside the blast zone. This gave rescue workers enough room to begin uncovering new layers of steel, concrete, and other debris lying on the ground in dangerously unstable piles. Some four hundred dogs trained to assist in rescues also took part in these efforts—the largest deployment of rescue dogs in history.

However, rescuers could not find many survivors—instead they found almost nothing but corpses. Only twenty people were pulled alive from the rubble, including six firefighters and three police officers.

Amid the havoc and heartache was one hopeful symbolic gesture. A few hours after the attack, three firefighters, standing on debris about twenty feet off the ground, raised an American flag on a pole they had found. It came from a yacht that had been moored nearby. The owner of the flag had cut it down and given it to one of the firefighters.

Continuing the Work

Once the immediate work of aiding victims was over, in the next weeks and months the job of clearing debris began. Heavy pieces of equipment, such as excavators and cranes, were used to dig out the rubble that filled huge holes or lay on the ground. As the operators of these machines worked, they uncovered not only remnants of the buildings but also the bodies of thousands more victims.

Most of the cleared debris was steel that had once been building material. As this steel was carefully removed from the site, volunteer ironworkers cut the twisted metal into manageable sizes. Then these pieces and other debris, such as pieces of what once were office walls, were trucked to a huge landfill on Staten Island. By May 2002, when the clearing operation officially came to an end, workers had moved some 108,000 truckloads of material weighing an estimated 1.8 million tons (1.6 million metric tons).

As the removal of debris continued, many other tasks required attention. One was to repair the severely damaged bathtub that kept river water from flooding the area. Another was to remove some two thousand cars trapped in the underground garage. These were a major

A firefighter stands in the middle of grotesquely twisted pieces of steel and other charred debris during cleanup efforts at the site of the terrorist attack on the World Trade Center. Approximately 1.8 million tons of debris was removed from the site.

hazard because their gasoline was highly flammable. Still another hazard was the potentially explosive 1.2 million rounds of ammunition in an underground vault belonging to law enforcement agencies.

One recovery effort was perhaps less dangerous, but it was nonetheless noteworthy. In the weeks after the disaster, workers removed $230 million in precious metals from a vault owned by a group of commercial banks. The vault had been in a basement level of Four World Trade Center, one of several nearby buildings damaged in the collapse of the towers.

Round-the-Clock Recovery Work

Since the beginning of the recovery efforts, the people of Manhattan had pitched in to do what they could to help. For example, local merchants donated food and water for the rescue and cleanup teams who were working around the clock. Construction projects around the city came to a halt as workers walked off their jobs to help.

Many firefighters and others worked weeks of round-the-clock, twelve-hour shifts on the rubble pile. Many of them took only brief naps, sleeping in a nearby church or even on nearby streets. All told, cleanup and recovery continued twenty-four hours a day over a period of eight months.

Other people who came to help were from all across the country and several other nations. Many of them took leaves of absence from their jobs, sometimes traveling at their own expense. In addition to everyday people, their ranks included professionals such as police officers, firefighters, disaster workers, and metalwork and construction experts.

The areas where they labored went far beyond the site of the towers themselves, because the crashes did not destroy only the Twin Towers. Debris from their collapse also severely damaged many buildings in the area. One of these was Seven World Trade Center, which burned for hours and was completely destroyed by 5:21 p.m. Although Seven World Trade Center and the Twin Towers were the largest buildings to suffer damage, many other nearby structures were also destroyed or damaged beyond repair. Among these were Three, Four, Five, and

ESCAPING

The towers had not been designed to facilitate mass evacuations. The elevators on the North Tower had shut down, so the stairs were the only option. But only three stairwells went all the way from top to bottom. Escape routes were fewer than within the Empire State Building, built in 1931. And the stairwells had no lighting, leaving evacuees in darkness. Furthermore, two stairways ended not on the ground level but on the mezzanine, half a story higher, and the mass of evacuees had to rush down still more stairs from the mezzanine in order to reach ground level.

Many people above the point of impact tried to reach the roof, only to find that the access doors were locked. Fleeing to the roof was a natural response, since people thought they would be rescued by helicopter. Journalists Tim Dwyer and Kevin Flynn note, "The roof offered fresh air. There was no ceiling to collapse, no furniture to burn, no floors to buckle. It seemed like a place removed from the hazard, a holding station that might buy time until rescuers arrived."

But even if they had been able to reach the roof, rescue was impossible. Several helicopters did try to land but were prevented because of thick smoke and flames. In fact, Joseph Esposito, the chief in charge of the police department's high-rise experts, ordered his pilots away by radio because he knew they would not survive.

Tim Dwyer and Kevin Flynn, *102 Minutes: The Untold Story of the Fight to Survive Inside the Twin Towers*. NY: Henry Holt, 2005, p. 129.

Six World Trade Center as well as a historic Greek Orthodox Church and skyscrapers such as the immense Deutsche Bank Building just off Wall Street. And the destruction spread much farther as well. In total, some eighteen thousand small businesses were destroyed or had to move because damage to their buildings was so extensive.

The Pile Becomes Ground Zero

For weeks after the attack, conditions at the crash site remained dreadful. The smoke and the smell of decaying human remains were overwhelming. Columns of twisted metal reached high above the street. On the ground, the piles of debris were still dangerously unstable and smoldering. As they worked, cleanup crews gave this nightmarish scene a name: "The Pile." Only later did it become known as Ground Zero.

A number of facilities were set up around the city to help in the aftermath of the disaster. For example, the US Navy medical support ship *Comfort* served as a 250-bed hospital facility and also provided respite for relief workers. Furthermore, over the course of a few weeks *Comfort* served some 17,000 meals to relief workers, provided shelter for 2,300 of them, and even cleaned 4,400 pounds of their laundry.

Another example of a facility that was used to aid people was the 69th Regiment Armory, a huge military building on Manhattan's Lexington Avenue. It was turned into a center for providing mental health counseling for survivors and their families as well as a hub for people searching for missing family and friends. People hoping to connect with survivors also posted thousands of photocopied posters of their missing loved ones. One eyewitness comments, "In the nearby area, you can't get away from faces of innocent victims who were killed. Their pictures are everywhere, on phone booths, street lights, walls of subway stations. Everything reminded me of a huge funeral, people quiet and sad, but also very nice. Before, New York gave me a cold feeling; now people were reaching out to help each other."[39]

The Terrorists

As the recovery process continued, the US government mounted an intense effort to answer one overwhelming question: Why did this happen? As the world knows now, the answer was terrorism.

When the first plane hit the North Tower, many people, both on the ground and in the towers, thought that it was an accident—a horrible accident, to be sure, but not deliberate. After all, airplanes had struck skyscrapers in years past. But when the second plane hit the South Tower, it became clear that this was a planned attack.

As the government soon learned, nineteen terrorists from an Islamist militant group had carried out this suicide mission. These terrorists were associated with a group called al Qaeda, and the organization's founder, Osama bin Laden, had masterminded the attack.

The World Trade Center strike was not the first made by al Qaeda against the United States. The organization had been behind the 1993 bombing of the building. It was also responsible for the bombings in 1998 of US embassies in the African nations of Tanzania and Kenya, in which hundreds of people had died. And it was behind a 2000 suicide attack on the USS *Cole* that killed seventeen American sailors when it was in port in Yemen, a nation in the Mideast.

Boarding the Planes

For years Bin Laden had been encouraging such missions against Americans as part of a holy war, asserting that dying in the cause of Islam guaranteed a place in heaven. He also passionately opposed what he saw as the Western world's corrupt nature.

After the World Trade Center attacks, Bin Laden stated that he had planned them specifically as retaliation for the United States' support of Israel, the presence in Saudi Arabia of American troops, and economic sanctions against the Middle Eastern country of Iraq. Paul Goldberger comments, "It is something of a paradox that the very things that attracted tourists to the World Trade Center—bigness, swagger, the sense that they embody the very force of capitalism—are the same things that led the terrorists to make the buildings their target."[40]

The terrorists chosen for the World Trade Center mission had trained for years to prepare themselves. Several spoke English, were well educated, and had lived in the west. These men entered the United States and took flying lessons so that they would be able to pilot the jets. They practiced portions of their plans for months before the attack, such as making dry runs of smuggling weapons onto a plane.

Early on the morning of September 11 they split up and boarded four commercial jets. Two of the flights originated in Boston,

Massachusetts; one from Newark, New Jersey; and one from Washington, DC.

The Hijacking

Although the weapons the terrorists carried were never exactly determined, they were probably high-strength metal folding utility knives, which at the time were not banned from commercial flights. Generally speaking, only guns, large knives, explosives, and incendiaries were prohibited. It was up to individual screening personnel to decide if some other kind of potential weapon was allowable.

In any case, all nineteen hijackers were able to pass successfully through the checkpoint screening to board their flights. A staff member for the official commission that later studied the disaster comments, "They were 19 for 19. They counted on beating a weak system."[41]

Once in the air the terrorists succeeded in taking over all four planes, forcing the crews to give up control. The hijackers aboard American Airlines Flight 11 and United Airlines Flight 93 were the ones who aimed their jets—which were now essentially guided missiles—toward the Twin Towers.

But the World Trade Center was not the only target that day. The two other planes headed toward the Washington, DC, area. One of them crashed into the Pentagon, the headquarters of the US military, which is located in Arlington, Virginia. The other plane was apparently aimed at the US Capitol Building, but it crashed in a field near Shanksville, Pennsylvania, when passengers prevented the hijackers from completing their plans.

The FAA Responds

Even before the hijacked planes struck their targets, the Federal Aviation Administration (FAA), which controls air traffic throughout the

Families and friends of people missing after the World Trade Center attacks posted thousands of photographs in hopes of finding their loved ones. Posters such as these appeared on phone booths, street lights, and subway station walls.

country, was aware that something was wrong. The planes were not on their scheduled routes. As standard procedure, the FAA had ordered military jets into the air to investigate. But the agency was not able to assess the situation before the planes reached their targets.

After the attacks, when it became clear that they were deliberate acts, the FAA took drastic action. It immediately grounded all commercial aircraft scheduled for takeoff in the continental United States—that is, the entire country except Hawaii and Alaska. Airplanes that were already in the air were instructed to make emergency landings. Jets in the air that belonged to airlines of other countries and had originated in the United States were ordered to return to America. And all international flights scheduled to come into the United States were canceled.

Other government agencies and officials besides the FAA responded quickly, suspecting that Islamist terrorists were behind the attacks. Within hours, the FBI released the names—and in many cases the personal details—of the suspected hijackers. By midday, intelligence agencies in the United States and Germany had intercepted communications pointing to Bin Laden. And by early afternoon US secretary of defense Donald Rumsfeld was issuing orders to look for specific evidence of involvement by Islamist terrorists headquartered in Iraq.

The nation—and the world—were still in shock. But there was also hope. An immediate and widespread outpouring of sympathy—everything from letters from children to billions of dollars in aid from the federal government and other countries—poured in. Donations of blood sharply increased around the country. And dozens of relief funds were set up to assist the families of victims of the attacks. These acts were only the beginning of extensive efforts to honor the dead and keep the memory of 9/11 alive.

CHAPTER FIVE

Rebuilding and Remembering

In the months following the disaster, outrage over the attack continued unabated throughout the world. The United Nations Security Council issued a resolution stating its readiness to combat all forms of terrorism. And many nations passed strict anti-terrorism legislation, froze bank accounts that were suspected to aid al Qaeda terrorists, and arrested alleged terrorists.

On a more personal scale, thousands of individuals overseas sent letters of support. Closer to home, an estimated 250 nonprofit organizations were established, dedicated to helping those affected and make sure victims were honored. Jay Winuk, cofounder of one of these organizations, MyGoodDeed, comments, "The amazing spirit of compassion and community service that grew out of 9/11 was so natural and evident immediately after the attacks."[42]

More Memorials

Meanwhile, many cities and organizations created memorials such as parks, benefit concerts, and annual observances. For example, at Ground Zero an installation of eighty-eight searchlights, the Tribute in Light, annually projects two vertical columns of light in remembrance. Only four months after the attack a US flag found at the site flew on the space shuttle *Endeavour* to the International

Space Station, and in the years since, astronauts have carried thousands more tributes into space. Another US flag, this one about 20 feet (6 m) high and 30.5 feet (9.3 m) wide, had been flying across the street from the World Trade Center at time of the attack. Shredded by the blasts, the flag was painstakingly repaired and sent on tour around the country as the "National 9/11 Flag." Yet another tribute involved the use of twenty-four tons (21.7 metric tons) of steel from the building's wreckage in the construction of a new naval ship, the USS *New York*. This ship, launched in 2008, was named to honor the memory of those who died in the World Trade Center attack.

But the most extensive memorial by far is a park on the site of Ground Zero. In 2003 over fifty-two hundred proposals from sixty-three nations were submitted to an international competition to design this park. The winners were architect Michael Arad and the landscape architecture firm of Peter Walker and Partners.

Their design, called "Reflecting Absence," symbolizes the emptiness, physical and emotional, left by the disaster. At the same time, the designers wanted to demonstrate that the city—and by extension America—remained strong. Arad comments, "We wanted to create a place that remarked on absence but also did so in a way that connected the site back into the life of the city. . . . I've compared it in the past to a moment of silence."[43]

"Reflecting Absence" occupies roughly half the 16-acre footprint (6.5 ha) of the original complex. It consists of a forest of some four hundred trees surrounding two enormous sunken pools over the exact footprints of the Twin Towers. The largest man-made waterfalls in the United States cascade down the sides of the pools. And the names of 2,983 people—including victims of the hijacked airplanes and the 1993 World Trade Center bombing—are inscribed on bronze plates attached to the edges of the pools' walls.

The memorial opened on September 11, 2011—exactly ten years after 9/11—for an invited group that included the families of victims. It opened to the general public the next day. In its first year alone, more than 4.6 million people visited to pay their respects.

Rebuilding

As plans for the memorial park moved forward, an even larger question was raised: What should be done about the site as a whole?

Authorities, the families of victims, and the public at large had widely differing feelings. Some passionately believed that the area was sacred and should remain undeveloped. Others felt that a new office complex was appropriate. They argued that rebuilding would be both economically and emotionally sensible. Mayor Rudy Giuliani—who had been widely praised for his leadership during the disaster—supported this idea. He had proclaimed on the day of the attack, "We will rebuild. We're going to come out of this stronger

On the five year anniversary of the 9/11 attacks, the Tribute in Light reaches to the heavens over the lower Manhattan skyline. The beacons of light pay tribute to the thousands who died and to the Twin Towers that were once a symbol of New York City.

than before, politically stronger, economically stronger. The skyline will be made whole again."[44]

After lengthy negotiations, a compromise was reached: A complex of new office buildings would be built. Its centerpiece was a skyscraper originally called Freedom Tower. This structure was renamed One World Trade Center because it was felt that the public would identify with the name more easily. Journalist Deepti Hajela writes, "To many, the [original] name conveyed resilience, even defiance. But others found it too provocative and worried that it could make the tower an even more tempting target for terrorists."[45]

Architect Daniel Libeskind won the competition held to create an overall plan for the project, and another architect, David Childs, was commissioned to design the skyscraper. The groundbreaking ceremony for the skyscraper took place on July 4, 2004, and as of early 2013 the building was scheduled for completion in 2014.

Analyzing Death and Destruction

As plans for rebuilding slowly became realities, experts pursued many other grim tasks. For one thing, intense efforts were made to discover exactly why the buildings collapsed. To make a forensic analysis of the disaster, a coalition of government agencies and private firms sifted through tons of recovered debris, examined hours of video footage shot from various angles, and studied hundreds of eyewitness accounts.

The task force came to a number of conclusions. Notably, it appeared that the towers might have remained standing if not for one crucial factor: The impact of the planes destroyed many of the exterior support columns on the floors that had been hit. By itself this might not have resulted in complete collapse. But the extreme heat of burning jet fuel caused other building material to buckle, in particular the internal box column and the system of shock absorbers supporting the floors. The buckling of the interior column and

WORDS IN CONTEXT

forensic
The application of science to legal problems.

74

GREEN AND SECURE

When completed—a task scheduled for 2014—One World Trade Center will be a sleek glass tower rising to a symbolic point: 1,776 feet (541.3 m), representing the year of America's independence. Five towers will range around it, and the entire complex will encompass some 3 million square feet (0.3 million square meters).

The complex will not only be massive, it will also be one of the most environmentally friendly buildings in the world. For example, to help make the building as "green" as possible, much of its construction material has been recycled from other buildings, and more than three-quarters of the waste it generates will be recycled. Furthermore, improvements in window technology will increase visibility and allow as much daylight in as possible, reducing the need for electric lighting.

As might be expected, security was a major concern during the design process. The skyscraper's 3-foot-thick concrete walls (1 m) are designed to withstand high winds and earthquakes, and its massive base includes blast-resistant walls. There are also state-of-the-art fire-suppression systems, seventy specially protected elevators, and a separate stairway to be used only by fire and safety personnel. Eduardo del Valle, a design consultant for the Port Authority, comments, "I can tell you that it may not be the tallest building in the world, but it is certainly the safest."

Quoted in Robert Sullivan, "A Look at the New One World Trade Center," *Architectural Digest*, September 2012. www.architecturaldigest.com.

shock absorbers twisted the support columns until they weakened and failed.

Some of the commission's conclusions pointed to inadequacies in New York City building codes at the time of the towers' construction. These codes were more lenient than those in place today. For example, they required only three exit stairwells for high-rise buildings. Remarkably, they also required no fire sprinkler systems except for underground spaces. After the 1993 attack the Port Authority began strengthening its safety measures, improving the sprinkler system and making other changes. But these efforts were slow to come and obviously proved inadequate.

Analysis of the buildings' collapse was not the only task needed— or perhaps even the most important one. A far more grim undertaking was to identify human remains, still an ongoing process. Soon after the disaster rescuers recovered the intact corpses of nearly three hundred victims as well as roughly 19,500 body parts. For years afterward human remains continued to be found both at Ground Zero and at the landfill where debris had been taken.

The job of matching these fragments to individuals is time consuming and difficult. Experts are using such techniques as DNA and dental records analysis. Sometimes personal effects such as jewelry and tattoos have been clues. But as of late 2012 only slightly more than half of the victims have been definitively matched with remains.

Health Issues

Not only did the disaster kill thousands of people outright, it affected countless more due to the toxic debris and smoke that spread across the city. These highly dangerous clouds contained an estimated twenty-five hundred contaminants, including cancer-causing agents such as asbestos. The extent of the toxicity was so severe that not until the summer of 2002 did the Environmental Protection Agency announce that the air quality had returned to levels before the attacks.

Exposure to this toxicity has created serious, long-term physical health problems, especially among people who spent time at Ground Zero during the rescue and recovery period. In the scramble to help, many did not have time to be outfitted with safety gear. For example, they frequently spent long periods without proper respirators.

As a result, reported health problems have been high. As of early 2013 an estimated eighteen thousand people had developed physical illnesses related to 9/11. For example, nearly every firefighter at the scene reported having breathing problems that they had never experienced before, and studies indicate that they have a significantly greater risk for developing cancer than American males in general.

Thousands of civilian volunteers were also affected. And many more may be diagnosed in the future, since they may not develop symptoms for years.

Local and federal agencies have tried to ease the problem through financial aid and other measures. For example, in 2011 President Barack Obama signed a bill that provides $4.2 billion toward testing and treatment for people suffering from long-term health problems related to 9/11.

Physical health damage is not the only lingering problem. The mental well-being of survivors, witnesses, and the families of victims has also been a particular concern. Not everyone exposed to disaster is traumatized, but the incidence in this case has been significant. Thousands of people, especially in the New York City area, have reported lingering emotional problems such as depression, anxiety, panic attacks, and post-traumatic stress disorder (PTSD).

All in all, the health problems caused by 9/11 have been severe. Thomas Farley, an official of the New York City Department

of Health and Mental Hygiene, comments, "More than a decade of studies suggest that while the majority of people exposed to the WTC [World Trade Center] disaster are healthy and symptom free, thousands of individuals—including rescue, recovery and clean-up workers and people who lived, worked or went to school in Lower Manhattan on 9/11—have developed chronic, and often co-occurring, mental and physical health conditions."[46]

On the other hand, the impact of 9/11 on the mental health of Americans overall may not be as permanent as some fear. People as a whole are remarkably resilient. One national study indicates that the general mental health of the country overall has not been permanently affected, and that it has survived the emotional strains of the disaster remarkably well. Speaking of this research, Roxanne Cohen Silver, a psychologist at the University of California, Irvine notes, "It became very clear after 9/11 that the impact of communal and

⬡ THE MUSEUM

A museum seventy feet below ground level is part of the overall plan for the tributes at Ground Zero for the victims of 9/11. The museum was originally scheduled to open in September 2009, but it has been delayed for years for several reasons. Notably, in 2011 political conflicts and funding problems halted construction for months. Also, Hurricane Sandy in October 2012 further hampered work, flooding the underground facility to a depth of seven feet. As of early 2013, the museum was scheduled to open in 2014. When completed it will house an estimated forty thousand artifacts, including a fire truck that responded to the event, personal mementos and photographs of the victims, and the last steel column removed from the site—a 58-ton piece (52.6 metric tons) more than 36 feet (11 m) tall.

collective trauma spilled over beyond the directly-impacted communities [but] in general, the message was one of resilience. . . . We saw normal reactions to an abnormal event."[47]

Backlash

In addition to the various mental and physical health problems caused by the disaster, the events of 9/11 have had countless other negative repercussions. One unfortunate example concerns backlash against Muslim communities in the United States. After the attacks the American public was understandably tense about the possibility of more to come, and there were many instances of fear-driven assaults or incidences of prejudice against Muslims—despite the fact that terrorists comprise only a tiny fraction of the religion's followers.

Hundreds of cases of anti-Muslim vandalism, arson, assault, harassment, and even murder have been reported since 9/11. In some cases anyone perceived to be Muslim has been a target, even if that person simply looked foreign. One well-publicized example came just days after 9/11, when a native of India who followed the Sikh faith was shot and killed in Arizona. Other similarly fatal mistakes include the murder in 2011 of two Sikh men in California and the 2012 slaying of six people at a Sikh temple in Wisconsin.

Although not always violent, bigotry against Muslims continues. In a Gallup survey conducted in 2010, nearly half of the Americans polled admitted to feeling at least "a little" prejudice toward Muslims—more than twice the number who say the same about Christians, Jews, or Buddhists. And in 2011 a survey by the Pew Research Center for the People and the Press, a majority of Muslims said the terrorist attacks made it more difficult to be a Muslim in the United States. Muslim respondents said they feel they are singled out by security officers and that people are suspicious of them or call them offensive names. On the other hand, in the same Pew Research Center survey, a significant percentage of Muslims stated that many Americans had been friendly toward them and showed no outward signs of prejudice.

One well-publicized controversy has been taking place in the very shadow of Ground Zero. For about two years before 9/11 members of New York City's Muslim community had used a building near the blast site for worship. During that time more ambitious plans were made to build an Islamic community center and mosque there. *New York Times* reporter Anne Bernard, writing in 2011, comments, "When the plans were announced last year, there were angry protests from some relatives of 9/11 victims, politicians and others who said it would be insensitive to build a Muslim institution close to where Islamic radicals attacked the World Trade Center on Sept. 11, 2001. The furor was fanned by Internet-based activists who viewed Muslim influence as a threat and called the project a "victory mosque."[48]

In the face of these protests, the supporters of the proposed community center have organized significant changes. For example, they have made strong efforts to include a wide variety of people, including the families of victims, in making decisions about the site. They have also planned exhibits commemorating the victims of the attacks. As of early 2013 they were hoping to reach a compromise with opponents.

The new skyscraper, One
World Trade Center
(originally known as the
Freedom Tower), forms the
centerpiece of a new complex
of buildings near the site
of the Twin Towers. In the
forefront of the photograph
is a sunken pool marking the
footprint of the lost towers.

Big Changes

In spite of such controversies, the work being done to rebuild the damaged area around Ground Zero has served as a reminder of the strength and determination of New York City and its people. Mayor Michael R. Bloomberg commented in 2012, "A crucial part of the story of September 11th is how Lower Manhattan—an area many people said would turn into a ghost town—has come back in the past 10 years. People from across the country and around the world have contributed to its revival, and now we want our visitors to see that full recovery for themselves. Lower Manhattan is where the first chapters in the remarkable story of New York City were written four hundred years ago. And it's where the next installment of New York City's story is being written today."[49]

The events of 9/11 have clearly had profound and long-lasting effects around the globe—indeed, many people have commented that the world changed forever on that day. Although Islamic terrorists had been carrying out strikes for many years beforehand, the sheer magnitude of the World Trade Center attacks made it clear that the terrorists were essentially at war. A few days after the attack, on September 14, President George W. Bush visited Ground Zero and told rescue workers, "It's hard to describe what it's like to see the gnarled steel and broken glass and twisted buildings silhouetted against the smoke. I said that this was the first act of war on America in the 21st century and I was right, particularly having seen the scene."[50]

Almost immediately the Bush administration launched a wide-ranging effort to revamp American intelligence and security efforts, shifting the emphasis toward stopping terrorism. On September 20 Bush, addressing the nation and Congress, outlined his administration's plans.

One major aspect of these plans was the USA PATRIOT Act. This law, which Congress quickly passed, gave the government broad powers in the name of gathering anti-terrorism intelligence. For example, the government was given the authority to detain foreign suspects for a week without charge, to monitor communication among suspects, and to prosecute suspected terrorists without time restrictions. This act has in the years since been the source of tremendous controversy. Notably, its critics charge that the act's broad powers in collecting information violate the US Constitution's guarantee of privacy and freedom of speech.

Homeland Security

Related to this sweeping law was the Homeland Security Act. This bill shifted the priorities of the government's law enforcement agencies, placing their primary emphasis on security against terrorists. One prominent example of this was the refocusing of FBI activity from domestic crime to the investigation of terrorist threats.

The Homeland Security Act also placed many agencies, such as the Immigration and Naturalization Service and the US Secret Service, within a huge new umbrella organization, the Department of Homeland Security (DHS). The American public immediately felt the effects of DHS's tightened measures. Well-known examples include rigorous security policies in airports and at border crossings.

The Bush administration did much more than authorize the restructuring of government agencies, however. Only about a month after the attacks, the president authorized the US military to lead a coalition of international forces in an attempt to overthrow a fundamentalist Islamic regime in Afghanistan because the country was harboring al Qaeda terrorists, including Osama bin Laden, the leader of the 9/11 attacks. This led to an extended conflict between the Taliban, the radical Islamist group that was controlling Afghanistan, and an American-led coalition of forces. As of early 2013 a small number of American troops were still in Afghanistan but were scheduled to leave within a year.

Meanwhile, the war on terror, as the Bush administration dubbed it, continued on another front. In 2003 the United States led an invasion and occupation of Iraq, with the Bush administration asserting that the Middle Eastern country also posed a threat to American security. US-led forces occupied Iraq for seven years until President Obama directed the departure of the last American soldiers in late

2011. And a major blow was dealt to al Qaeda when American forces tracked down and killed the mastermind of the 9/11 attacks, Osama bin Laden, in 2011. In announcing this event, President Obama commented, "Tonight, let us think back to the sense of unity that prevailed on 9/11. I know that it has, at times, frayed. Yet today's achievement is a testament to the greatness of our country and the determination of the American people."[51]

The president's comments reflect the efforts that are being made to ensure that the nation will never forget the events of 9/11, despite the controversies that have sometimes ensued. In fact, the World Trade Center was controversial from the very beginning, and this criticism continued throughout the years of its original design and construction. But the project survived this strong opposition and although it was still disliked by many it became a familiar sight and a dramatic symbol of New York City and of the United States itself. Following the attacks of 2001, the structures—or, more accurately, the absence of the structures—have taken an even more prominent place in the public eye. Whatever the future holds for the buildings that have taken the place of the original structures, the Twin Towers will remain an indelible part of history.

SOURCE NOTES

Introduction: An American Icon

1. Quoted in Camilo Jose Vergara, *Twin Towers Remembered*. New York: Princeton Architectural Press, 2001, p. 1.
2. Camilo Jose Vergara, *Twin Towers Remembered*. New York: Princeton Architectural Press, 2001, p. 3.

Chapter One: Why the World Trade Center Was Built

3. Karl Koch III, *Men of Steel: The Story of the Family That Built the World Trade Center*. NYC: Crown, 2002, p. 173.
4. Roger Cohen, "Casting Giant Shadows: The Politics of Building the World Trade Center," *Portfolio: A Quarterly Review of Trade and Transportation, Winter 1990–91*. www.greatbuildings.com.
5. Cohen, "Casting Giant Shadows."
6. Bill Harris, *World Trade Center: A Tribute*. Philadelphia: Courage Books, 2001, p. 26.
7. Anthony Robins, *Classics of American Architecture: The World Trade Center*. Englewood, FL: Pineapple Press, 1987, p. 21
8. Quoted in PBS, *American Experience: The Center of the World*, "Biography: David and Nelson Rockefeller." www.pbs.org.
9. Quoted in Bill Harris, *World Trade Center*, p. 8.
10. Quoted in Angelo Lomeo, Sonja Bullaty, and Paul Goldberger, *The World Trade Center Remembered*. New York: Abbevile, 2001, p. 22.
11. Quoted in Marc Pitzke, "'Who's Afraid of the Big, Bad Buildings?' How New Yorkers Tried to Stop the World Trade Center," *Spiegel* (Germany) *Online International*, September 8, 2011. www. spiegel.de.
12. Quoted in Joseph Giovanni, "Fixing the Whole," *New York Magazine*, November 12, 2001. http://nymag.com.

13. Eric Darton, *Divided We Stand: A Biography of New York's World Trade Center.* New York: Basic Books, 1999, p. 74.

14. Martin Arnold, "High Court Plea Is Lost by Foes of World Trade Center," *New York Times*, November 13, 1963. www.nytimes.com.

15. Quoted in Edith Evans Asbury, "Downtown Merchants Parade to Protest World Trade Center," *New York Times*, July 14, 1962. www.nytimes.com.

16. Quoted in Asbury, "Downtown Merchants Parade to Protest World Trade Center."

17. Quoted in Darton, *Divided We Stand*, p. 132.

Chapter Two: The World Trade Center Takes Shape

18. Darton, *Divided We Stand*, p. 16.

19. Koch, *Men of Steel*, pp. 193–94.

20. Quoted in Robins, *Classics of American Architecture*, p. 32.

21. Leslie E. Robertson, "Reflections on the World Trade Center," *National Academy of Engineering*, Spring 2002. www.nae.edu.

22. Koch, *Men of Steel*, p. 244.

23. Harris, *World Trade Center*, p. 55.

24. Koch, *Men of Steel*, pp. 251–53.

25. Quoted in Harris, *World Trade Center*, p. 55.

Chapter Three: An Instant Icon

26. Kari Haskell, "Before & After; Talking of the Towers," *New York Times*, September 16, 2001.

27. Quoted in Koch, *Men of Steel*, p. 200.

28. Quoted in Robins, *Classics of American Architecture*, p. 50.

29. Robins, *Classics of American Architecture*, p. 58.

30. Quoted in Haskell, "Before & After; Talking of the Towers."

31. Quoted in Sam Moses, "The Only Way to Go Is Up," *Sports Illustrated*, June 6, 1977. http://sportsillustrated.cnn.com.

32. Moses, "The Only Way to Go Is Up."

33. PBS, "Tightrope Between the Towers," *American Experience*. www.pbs.org.

34. Quoted in Claudine Zap, "'Man on Wire' Remembers Twin Towers," *Yahoo News*, August 15, 2011. http://news.yahoo.com.

35. Darton, *Divided We Stand*, p. 119.

36. Federal Bureau of Investigation, "FBI 100: First Strike: Global Terror in America," *Stories*, February 26, 2008. www.fbi.gov.

Chapter Four: Death and Destruction

37. Quoted in Jason Samenow, "9/11 Weather: 2012 Conditions Closely Resemble 2001," *Washington Post*, September 11, 2012. www.washingtonpost.com.

38. Quoted in Tim Dwyer and Kevin Flynn, *102 Minutes: The Untold Story of the Fight to Survive Inside the Twin Towers*. NYC: Henry Holt, 2005, p. 64.

39. Quoted in Pete Sigmund, "Crews Assist Rescuers in Massive WTC Search," *Construction Equipment Guide*. www.constructionequipmentguide.com.

40. Quoted in Lomeo, *The World Trade Center Remembered*, p. 14.

41. Quoted in CNN News, "9/11 Panel: Hijackers May Have Used Utility Knives," January 27, 2004. http://articles.cnn.com.

Chapter Five: Rebuilding and Remembering

42. Quoted in CBS New York, "Volunteers Honor 9/11 Victims by Helping Others on National Day Of Service," September 11, 2012. http://newyork.cbslocal.com.

43. Quoted in Jessica Dailey, "The National 9/11 Memorial Is Now Open in NYC," *Inhabitat New York City*, September 11, 2012. http://inhabitat.com.

44. Quoted in Tess Taylor, "Rebuilding in New York," *Architecture Week*, October 3, 2001. www.architectureweek.com.

45. Quoted in Deepti Hajela, "Freedom Tower? One World Trade Center? What Do You Call It?," *Huffington Post*, June 16, 2012. www.huffingtonpost.com.

46. Quoted in NYC.gov, "What We Know About the Health Effects of 9/11." www.nyc.gov.

47. Quoted in Melanie Nayer, "9/11 Anniversary: 10 Years Later, Tourists Check-In to Lower Manhattan." *Huffington Post*, September 8, 2012. www.huffingtonpost.com.

48. Anne Bernard, "Developers of Islamic Center Try a New Strategy," *New York Times*, August 1, 2011.

49. Quoted in Nayer, "9/11 Anniversary."

50. Quoted in Elisabeth Bumiller, "Two Strangers, Bush and New York City, Meet and Embrace in Calamity's Wake," *New York Times*, September 15, 2001. http://tv.nytimes.com.

51. Quoted in *Huffington Post*, "Osama bin Laden Dead, Obama Announces," May 1, 2011. www.huffingtonpost.com.

FACTS ABOUT THE WORLD TRADE CENTER

Work and Visitors
- Number working in Twin Towers on average day before 9/11: 50,000.
- Average number of daily visitors to observation deck before 9/11: 80,000.

Construction
- Height: North Tower, including antenna: 1,730 feet (527 m) (including antenna).
- South Tower: 1,362 feet (415 m).
- Number of stories: 110.
- Number of elevators per tower: 99.
- Length of heating ducts per tower: 198 miles (318.6 km).
- Available office space on each floor: about 0.75 acres (0.3 ha).
- Number of doorknobs in Twin Towers: 42,000.
- Total length of cables in Twin Towers: 12,000 miles (19,300 km).
- Number of individual pieces of steel in Twin Towers: more than 200,000.
- Weight of each tower: 500,000 tons (446,428 metric tons).

9/11
- Number of fatalities, including passengers in jets: 2,977.
- Distance from which the burning towers were visible: about 20 miles (32 km).
- Maximum heat of fires: 2,300°F (1,260°C).
- Number of days that workers dug up debris at Ground Zero, searching for body parts: 230.
- Number of hot meals served to rescue workers: 343,000.
- Number of body parts collected: 19,500.
- Number of bodies discovered intact: 291.
- Number of orphans created by the 9/11 attacks: about 1,300.

The New Buildings

- Amount of office space in new One World Trade Center tower: 2.6 million square feet (241,547 square meters).
- Actual tower height: 1,368 feet (416.9 m); with antenna: 1,776 feet (541.3 m).
- Number of stories: 69.
- Amount of water flowing over memorial walls: 26,000 gal. (98,420 L) per minute.

FOR FURTHER RESEARCH

Books

Peter Benoit, *September 11,2001: We Will Never Forget*. NY: Children's, 2011.

Craig E. Bloehm, *The 9/11 Investigation*. Farmington Hills, MI: Lucent, 2009.

Don Brown, *America Is Under Attack: September 11, 2001: The Day the Towers Fell*. Crescent City, CA: Flash Point, 2011.

Philippe Petit, *Man on Wire*. NY: Skyhorse, 2008.

John Sterngrass, *Terrorism*. Tarrytown, NY: Marshall Cavendish, 2011.

Alan Wachtel, *September 11: A Primary Source History*. NY: Gareth Stevens, 2009.

Websites

9/11 (www.newyorker.com/online/blogs/photobooth/911). A series of photos in the *New Yorker*'s "Photo Booth" feature that were taken before, on, and after the day of the disaster.

9/11 Memorial (www.911memorial.org). The official site of the memorial at Ground Zero.

1 WTC Construction Time-Lapse Video (www.huffingtonpost .com/2012/04/26/1-wtc-construction-time-lapse-video_n_1455826 .html). A time-lapse record of the construction of the new One World Trade Center, provided by the *Huffington Post*.

Terrorism Research Information (http://cjc.delaware.gov/terrorism /history.shtml). This site, maintained by the Delaware Criminal Justice Council, has extensive information on the history and other aspects of global terrorism.

World Trade Center (www.wtc.com). The official website of the World Trade Center, this has extensive information about the site, especially the new construction.

World Trade Center (www.panynj.gov/wtcprogress/index.html). This site, maintained by the Port Authority of New York and New Jersey, provides a great deal of information about construction of the new World Trade Center, including a live webcam and a stomach-dropping video of construction workers high atop the tower.

INDEX

ABOUT THE AUTHOR

Adam Woog is the author of many books for children, young adults, and adults. He also teaches in a preschool. Woog and his wife live in Seattle, Washington, and have an adult daughter.